JANA

JESUS REVEALED in Bible Stories

FOR TEEN GIRLS

Real Biblical Stories to Find Your Identity in Christ, Navigate Teen Life with Resilience, and Step Into Your Purpose

ISBN 978-1-918150-04-9 (Paperback)
ISBN 978-1-918150-05-6 (Hardback)

Up Itchen Books
Visit us at upitchenbooks.com
Contact us at info@upitchenbooks.com

It is the Spirit who gives life; the flesh profits nothing. The words that I speak to you are spirit, and they are life.

John 6:63

Contents

Intro

The Bible is the only book in the world that reads you while you read it. It may look like a collection of ancient stories, but the moment you open it, you realize it is breathing. It offers you a reflection of your own soul. It is a mirror.

If you look closely enough, you will find every version of yourself hidden in its pages. You will find the person you were: the one who made mistakes, hid in shame, or felt unworthy. You will find the person you currently are: navigating stress, trying to fit in, or wondering if you have a purpose. And, most importantly, you will find the person you want to be: brave, influential, humble, and radiantly alive.

The good, the bad, the messy, and the miraculous; it's all there. This is the marvel of Scripture. It is alive. As 2 Timothy 3:16-17 tells us, God's Word is "breathed out" by God. It is the foremost manual for life. It is designed to teach, correct, train, and equip you so that you are ready for absolutely anything.

That is why this book is in your hands. This is a collection of 25 brilliant, captivating retellings of women and men who walked the same earth you walk. As you journey through their stories, you will find the tools to navigate the chaos of your teenage years, the pressure, the noise, and the relationships, with wisdom rather than fear.

But this book goes deeper than just survival; it is about finding your true identity in Christ. By seeing how God used these imperfect people, you will begin to see how He sees you: not as a victim of your circumstances, but as a daughter of the King. You will learn how to be intentional about your life, moving from where you are to where you want to be, making determined choices to grow, improve, and advance in your faith.

While we will look at 25 different people, there is really only one hero in this book. His name is Jesus.

One of the main visions of this book is for you to discover Jesus in places you never expected. We call this the **Messianic Thread**. Think of it like a movie trailer or a silhouette. The Old Testament characters are often types and shadows that give us a hint of what the Savior looks like. We highlight how that specific character points to the Messiah, helping you see the Bible as one unified story. By finding Him in their stories, you will learn to find your own purpose in Him.

HOW TO USE THIS BOOK

This book is designed to fit into your routine. You can use it as a daily devotional to set your mind right before school, or as a resource to flip through when you need specific encouragement. Each chapter is crafted to take just 10-15 minutes to read and digest, that's short enough to fit into a break, but deep enough to shift your perspective for the whole day.

To help you get the most out of these stories, every chapter comes with a toolkit designed to help you level up:

- **THE DOWNLOAD** This is the breakdown. We take the drama of the story and highlight the key learning points that relate to your actual life right now.
- **REFLECT** You cannot grow if you are not honest. The Bible places a huge importance on self-examination. This section helps you check your GPS, seeing where you are versus where God wants you to go.
- **MICRO-HABIT** Inspiration without action is just a daydream. This section gives you a small, practical step to take responsibility and make conscious changes, one step at a time.
- **MY PRAYER & AFFIRMATION** Scripture declares that death and life are in the power of the tongue. Your words have the power to shape your reality. This is where you vocalize your faith. We do not beg God for things He has already given us; we thank Him for them. This is your opportunity to practice the power of a grateful heart.
- **REFERENCE SCRIPTURE & GET MORE** Don't just take my word for it. This book is the appetizer, but the Bible is the main course. Use these references to read the full story for yourself.

So... The world is going to throw a lot at you. There will be pressure and noise. But with God's Word formed in your heart as a solid foundation, you will become resilient to the wiles of the devil. You will stop being a victim of your circumstances and start being a victor over them.

CHAPTER 1

Eve

SEEING BEYOND THE PHYSICAL

> *No temptation has overtaken you except such as is common to man; but God is faithful, who will not allow you to be tempted beyond what you are able, but with the temptation will also make the way of escape, that you may be able to bear it.*
>
> **1 Corinthians 10:13**

"Did He actually say that?"

The question hung in the humid air of the garden, slippery and cool like the creature winding around the branch. Eve paused. A moment ago, her mind had been clear, her purpose simple. Now, a fog was rolling in.

She looked at the fruit. It wasn't ugly. It wasn't rotting or terrifying. It was beautiful. It was sleek, heavy with juice, and the light caught its skin in a way that made her mouth water. It looked... good. And that was the confusing part. How could something that looked so right be so wrong?

You won't die, the voice hissed, smooth and logical. *God knows that when you eat of it, your eyes will be opened, and you will be like God.*

Eve glanced back at Adam. He was standing right there, silent, watching her. He wasn't stopping her.

The weight of her influence pressed on her shoulders, though she didn't realize it yet. If she took a bite, he would too.

She looked back at the fruit. The desire wasn't just for the taste; it was for the upgrade. She wanted to be smart. She wanted to be in control. She wanted to know what God knew. The restriction felt like God was holding out on her, like He didn't actually want her to be happy.

She reached out. The skin of the fruit was cool against her palm. *Just one bite. What's the worst that could happen?*

CRUNCH.

The flavor was electric, but the aftertaste was ash.

In a split second, the lights went out. The glory that had covered her skin like a shimmering robe vanished. Suddenly, the warm breeze felt biting. She looked at Adam, and for the first time in her existence, she felt the hot, prickly flush of shame. She was naked. She was exposed.

"Cover yourself," she gasped, scrambling for fig leaves, her fingers fumbling, tearing at the rough greenery to hide the skin she used to love.

Then came the sound. The footsteps. Usually, the sound of God walking in the garden was the best part of the day, a time for walks and talks. Now, it sounded like thunder.

"Where are you?"

They huddled in the bushes, trembling. When God finally drew them out, the blame spilled out of her mouth before she could stop it. "The serpent deceived me, and I ate." It wasn't my fault. It was the snake. It was the situation. It was the pressure.

God looked at them. The heartbreak in His eyes was worse than any anger. He spoke the consequences, and they were heavy. Pain. Toil. Separation.

But then, He did something unthinkable. He didn't leave them in their flimsy, scratching fig leaves. God took an innocent animal and ended its life. He skinned it. And with His own hands, the hands that shaped the mountains, He gently dressed Eve in the warm, durable skin.

He covered her shame, even though she had caused it.

THE DOWNLOAD

If sin looked like a monster, we'd all run away. But it doesn't. The trap of "good-looking" sin is real. The fruit was pleasing to the eye. In our world, that looks like the popular friend group that we know is toxic but makes us feel important, or the gossip that feels so good to share because it makes us the center of attention. Just because it looks good or feels good doesn't mean it isn't poison.

Eve's story is a great lesson in guarding your mind. The enemy didn't attack her with a sword; he attacked with a question: "Did God really say?" He made her question God's goodness. Every time you think, "God's instructions are just to ruin my fun," that is the same ancient lie.

When we miss the mark, we must refuse the urge to hide or shift the blame. Adam blamed Eve;

Eve blamed the serpent. But notice God's response? He provided a covering.

MESSIANIC THREAD God had to kill an animal to cover Eve's physical nakedness. Thousands of years later, God allowed His Son, the Lamb of God, to be killed to cover our spiritual nakedness. God covers our shame. We don't have to hide in the bushes anymore. We are clothed in righteousness because of Jesus.

REFLECT

What is one area of your life where you feel like God is holding out on you?

....

....

....

Did God really say? What is a lie about yourself or God that you have been believing lately?

....

....

....

How do you usually react when you get caught doing something wrong? Do you own it, or do you look for someone to blame?

....

....

....

MICROHABIT

- ❒ The next time you are about to do something you're unsure about (send a risky text, buy something you can't afford, join in on a mean joke), physically stop. Count to five. Ask yourself: "Does this look good, or is it actually good?"

MY PRAYER

Dear Father, I thank You that You have given me eyes that allow me to see the world through Your truth. I am filled with divine wisdom and discernment, and I am sensitive to Your voice above all others. I walk in the light of Your Word, easily recognizing and rejecting every deception, fully confident in Your goodness. Amen.

Get More

Genesis 3:1-21

CHAPTER 2

Sarah

YOU CAN TAKE GOD'S WORD TO THE BANK

> *But those who wait on the LORD Shall renew their strength; They shall mount up with wings like eagles, They shall run and not be weary, They shall walk and not faint.*
>
> **Isaiah 40:31**

It was too hot to be inside the tent, but Sarah stayed in the shadows anyway. She was ninety years old. Her skin, once smooth and celebrated in Pharaoh's court, was now mapped with deep lines of a life lived in the desert wind.

She listened to the voices outside. Abraham was talking to three strangers.

"Where is Sarah your wife?" one of them asked.

Sarah froze. Why were they asking about her? She pressed her ear against the heavy fabric of the tent wall.

"I will surely return to you about this time next year," the stranger said, his voice carrying a weight that made the air hum. "And Sarah your wife shall have a son."

A sound escaped Sarah's lips. It was a laugh.

It wasn't a happy laugh. It was a dry, cynical chuckle. A son? Now? After her body had ceased to be like that of a woman? After decades of crying into her pillow? After the absolute disaster that happened when she tried to take matters into her own hands with Hagar?

She remembered that mess vividly. Over thirteen years ago, she had panicked. She thought God needed help keeping His promise, so she gave her servant Hagar to Abraham. It had torn their family apart, creating jealousy, bitterness, and a rift that still stung. That was what happened when she tried to control the narrative.

And now this stranger says she's going to have a baby? At ninety?

"Why did Sarah laugh?" The voice outside was sharp now. "Is anything too hard for the Lord?"

Sarah's heart slammed against her ribs. She shrank back. "I didn't laugh," she lied, fear spiking in her chest.

"No, but you did laugh," He replied. He knew. He heard the doubt in her heart that she hadn't even spoken aloud.

She sat down on the rug, trembling. *Is anything too hard for the Lord?* She looked at her wrinkled hands. Logic said yes. Biology said yes. But the God who called them out of Ur... He said no.

A year later, the tent was filled with a sound that Sarah never thought she'd hear. The cry of a newborn.

She looked down at the baby boy wrapped in swaddling cloths. His skin was new; hers was old. The impossible had happened. Abraham, a centenarian, was beaming. They named him Isaac.

Isaac means *Laughter*.

God had taken her cynical, doubting laugh and turned it into a laugh of pure, delirious joy. She had waited a lifetime. She had messed up. She had doubted. But God had kept His word.

THE DOWNLOAD

We hate waiting. If the WiFi takes more than three seconds to load, we freak out. Now imagine waiting 25 years for a promise. That was Sarah.

Sarah's story hits us hard because we all have a Hagar plan. That's what happens when we give up on waiting for God and decide to force the outcome ourselves. Maybe you manipulate a situation to get someone to notice you, or you cheat to get the grade because you don't trust your studying. Worry and control are sisters. When we worry God won't come through, we try to take control, and we usually make a mess.

But here is the beautiful truth: God is bigger than your doubt. Sarah laughed at God! He didn't strike her with lightning. He called her out on it to restore her faith, and He still gave her the baby. Your questions do not cancel God's plans.

Sarah teaches us that true patience is an active expectation. It is the refusal to settle for a "good enough" solution when God has promised the best. We look to Sarah not just for her loyalty, but for her eventual faith. Hebrews 11 tells us that by faith, she received strength to conceive because she judged Him faithful who had promised.

MESSIANIC THREAD Sarah gave birth to a child of promise when her body was *dead* (barren and old). This points directly to the Gospel, where God brings life out of death. It also points to the Virgin Mary, for whom God did the impossible again.

REFLECT

What is your Isaac? What's the thing you are desperately waiting for right now?

....

....

....

Describe a time you tried to help God out (like Sarah with Hagar) and it backfired.

....

....

....

Is anything too hard for the Lord? Apply this question to your biggest current problem. What is the answer?

....

....

....

MICROHABIT

- [ ] Find a small box or a jar. Write down the one thing you are stressed about or trying to control on a slip of paper. Fold it up and put it in the box. Every time you worry about it, look at the box and say, "That's in God's box, not on my shoulders."

MY AFFIRMATION

I walk by faith and not by sight! I refuse to be moved by timelines, delays, or natural impossibilities. I judge God faithful, and I know that what He has said, He is able to perform. My strength is renewed daily, and I possess the endurance to see every promise manifested in my life. Hallelujah!

Get More

Genesis 18:1-15, Genesis 21:1-7

CHAPTER 3

Lot's Wife

WITHSTANDING THE LURE OF THE WORLD

But Jesus said to him, "No one, having put his hand to the plow, and looking back, is fit for the kingdom of God."

Luke 9:62

"Don't look back! Don't stop! Run for the hills or you will be swept away!"

The angels' voices were shouting over the roar of the city. It was chaos. Lot was stumbling, half-dazed. His wife grabbed her daughters' hands, her fingernails digging into their palms.

The angels seized Lot's hand, his wife's hand, and the hands of his two daughters. They were being physically dragged out of Sodom.

The sky was turning a sickly, bruising purple. The air smelled of sulfur and burning tar.

Run.

She ran. Her lungs burned. Her sandals slapped against the hard earth of the valley floor. But with every step away from the city, her heart felt like it was tearing in two.

She knew Sodom was bad. She knew it was wicked. But it was home. It was where her friends were. It was where she had hosted parties, bought fine linens, and established a reputation. It was where her life made sense. The mountains ahead looked dark, empty, and lonely.

Flee the sin! the angels had said.

But she didn't just see sin back there. She saw her comfort. She saw the things that defined her.

Hesitation is dangerous. She slowed her pace. Just a fraction.

I'll just take one look, she thought. *Just to say goodbye. Just to see if it's really happening.*

It wasn't just curiosity; it was attachment to the world. She wanted to see what she was leaving behind more than she wanted to see where God was taking her. She didn't take the warning seriously. Surely God wouldn't destroy it all?

She stopped. She turned her head.

The flash was blinding. Fire rained down from the heavens, consuming the city in an instant. But she didn't have time to scream.

The judgment caught her in the position of her heart: facing backward.

Her feet hardened. Her skin turned to grain. The salt of the Dead Sea valley encased her, freezing her forever in a pillar of white crystal. She was almost safe. She was almost out. But *almost* is the saddest word in the world.

THE DOWNLOAD

This is a heavy story. It's a tragedy. Lot's wife doesn't even get a name in the Bible, but Jesus specifically tells us later: "Remember Lot's wife."

Why? Because she represents a struggle we all have. Trust means not looking back.

Consider your own life. You decide to leave a toxic friend group, but you keep checking their social media to see what you are missing. You decide to speak words of life, but you keep listening to music that glorifies dysfunction. You physically leave the *Sodom* of your old habits, but your mind is still camping there.

Lot's wife teaches us that obedience is for your protection. God wasn't trying to be bossy when He said "Don't look back." He was trying to keep her from being consumed. When the Word instructs you to flee from immorality or step away from compromising situations, God is not trying to ruin your fun. He is protecting your destiny.

She hesitated. When God says move, you move. Delayed obedience is disobedience. If you linger in the doorway of a burning building, you're going to get burned.

MESSIANIC THREAD We need a Savior who drags us out of danger even when we drag our feet. But we also have a responsibility to follow. We cannot walk with Jesus while looking over our shoulder at the world. You can't have both.

REFLECT

What is something from your past (a habit, a relationship, a mistake) that you keep looking back at?

....

....

....

Why do you think it's so hard to let go of things we know are bad for us?

....

....

....

Almost saved. How does that phrase make you feel?

....

....

....

MICROHABIT

❒ Is there an app, a follow, or a text thread that represents your "Sodom": something toxic you keep going back to? This week, delete it. Unfollow. Block. Don't just hide it; remove the access. Don't look back.

MY AFFIRMATION

Father, I thank You that You have delivered me from the domain of darkness and transferred me into the Kingdom of Your Son. I am a new creation; the old life is dead, and the new has come. I refuse to look back at what I have left behind. I do not long for the comforts of compromise. My eyes are fixed forward on the high calling of God in Christ Jesus. I press on with singular focus. Hallelujah!

Get More

Genesis 19:12-26

CHAPTER 4

Leah

UNNOTICED BUT CHOSEN

> *For the LORD does not see as man sees; for man looks at the outward appearance, but the LORD looks at the heart.*
>
> ***1 Samuel 16:7***

The morning light in the tent was cruel. It illuminated everything Leah didn't want to see: the disappointment in Jacob's eyes when he woke up and realized he had married the wrong sister.

"It is I," she whispered, clutching the blankets.

He didn't yell. He didn't strike her. He just looked at her with a hollowness that hurt worse than a slap. He looked at her and wished she was Rachel. Everyone always wished she was Rachel. Rachel had the sparkling eyes and the figure that stopped traffic at the well. Leah had weak eyes. They were soft, ordinary, forgettable.

For years, Leah lived in the shadow of her sister's beauty. Now, she lived in the shadow of her husband's indifference. She was the wife by her father's trickery, not by her husband's choice.

If I just give him a son, she thought, desperation clawing at her chest, *then he will love me.*

So she bore a son. Reuben. "Surely now my husband will love me," she said.

But Jacob's eyes stayed fixed on Rachel's tent.

She bore another. Simeon. "Because the Lord heard I was unloved."

Still, Jacob was distant.

She bore a third. Levi. "Now at last my husband will be attached to me."

The silence in the camp remained deafening.

Leah was running a race she couldn't win. She was trying to buy affection with her body, trying to earn worth through performance. She measured her value by the attention of a man who couldn't see past the surface. Comparison was killing her contentment. Every time she looked at Rachel, she saw what she wasn't.

But then, something shifted.

When the fourth son came, Leah didn't look at Jacob. She didn't look at Rachel. She looked up. She stopped the exhausting hustle for validation. She realized that while her husband might not have chosen her, the God of the Universe had. God saw her tears. God saw her "weak eyes" and He looked deeper.

She held the baby boy and whispered a new declaration. She didn't mention Jacob. She didn't mention her pain.

"This time," she said, her voice steady with a new kind of strength, "I will praise the Lord."

She named him Judah. *Praise.*

She stopped asking a human being to fill a God-sized hole in her heart. She realized she was the underdog, yes, but God uses the underdog. She wasn't the pretty one but she was the ancestral mother of kings.

THE DOWNLOAD

We have all felt the sting of being the second choice. Maybe you weren't the one asked to prom. Maybe you weren't selected for the varsity team. Perhaps you were overlooked for a leadership role you thought you deserved, or you constantly feel overshadowed by a friend who seems to have the perfect life and the perfect look.

Leah teaches us a brutal but beautiful lesson: Human validation is not the metric of your worth. The world insists you must be visually striking to be valuable. That is a lie. Jacob might have wanted the beauty, but God wanted the heart.

Leah spent years miserable because she was seeking validation from people. She thought, "If I achieve this, if I look like this, then I'll be happy." It never works. The goalposts always move.

The turning point of her life was when she stopped saying, "Notice me, Jacob," and started saying, "Thank You, God."

MESSIANIC THREAD Jacob ignored Leah. He obsessed over Rachel and her son Joseph. But guess which son Jesus came from? Jesus, the Lion of the Tribe of Judah. The Savior of the world didn't come from the line of the beautiful, popular favorite. He came from the line of the unloved woman with the weak eyes who learned to praise God in her pain.

REFLECT

Who is the Rachel you constantly compare yourself to? What do you think she has that you lack?

....

....

....

Leah's name for Judah meant Praise. What is one struggle in your life right now that you can choose to praise God through?

....

....

....

How would your life change if you truly believed you were already chosen by God and didn't need to earn it?

....

....

....

MICROHABIT

- ❒ Catch yourself today. When you post a photo or walk into a room, ask yourself: "Am I doing this to get a reaction from others?" If the answer is yes, stop. Take 30 seconds to list three things God loves about you that have nothing to do with your appearance.

MY AFFIRMATION

Father, I thank You that I am hand-picked by You. I thank You that my value is not determined by the opinions of others, my appearance, or my relationship status. I am the righteousness of God in Christ, and I am complete in Him. I refuse to chase the wind of human approval. I break every agreement with rejection and comparison. I possess the spirit of praise, and like Leah, I lift my eyes to You. I am chosen, I am loved, and I am established. Hallelujah!

Get More

Genesis 29:16-35

CHAPTER 5

Joseph

GOD'S PLAN IS THE BEST PLAN

And we know that all things work together for good to those who love God, to those who are the called according to His purpose.

Romans 8:28

The pit was dark, dusty, and smelled of fear. Joseph looked up at the sliver of blue sky, the only connection to the world where he used to be the favorite son. He could hear his brothers eating lunch above him. They were laughing.

Just hours ago, he had been wearing the technicolor masterpiece of a coat that screamed "Dad loves me best." Now, it was torn off, and he was sold like cattle to a caravan of Ishmaelites.

It wasn't fair. He had done nothing wrong but share a dream God gave him.

Joseph was dragged to Egypt. He was stripped of his identity. He wasn't a son anymore; he was a slave. But Joseph made a choice. He couldn't control his location, but he could control his attitude. In Potiphar's house, he didn't pout; he worked. He worked so hard and with such excellence that he ran the whole estate. He bloomed where he was planted.

Then came the lie. Potiphar's wife accused him, and he was thrown into prison. Another pit. Another injustice.

Years passed. He could have sat in that cell and let bitterness destroy the vessel. He could have plotted revenge. He could have hated God. Instead, he ran the prison. He served the other prisoners. He kept his heart soft.

Fast forward. Joseph is the Prime Minister of Egypt. He is the second most powerful man in the world. Famine has ravaged the land, and ten desperate men stand before him, begging for grain.

His brothers. The ones who threw him away.

Joseph had the power to kill them with a snap of his fingers. He could have made them suffer. But when he looked at them, he didn't see enemies. He saw the pen of God writing a larger story.

He wept so loudly the Egyptians heard him.

"Do not be distressed," he told his terrified brothers. "You meant it for evil against me, but God meant it for good."

He chose to release the debt. He understood that forgiveness is a choice, not a feeling. He saw that the pit, the slavery, the prison, was all a setup to save the world from starvation.

THE DOWNLOAD

Joseph's life was a roller coaster of trauma. Betrayal, human trafficking, false accusation, imprisonment. If anyone had a right to be a victim, it was him.

But Joseph teaches us about God's perspective on pain. We look at a missed opportunity, a failed test, or a rumor and say, "This is a disaster." God looks at it and says, "This is development."

Joseph also masters the art of fleeing temptation. When Potiphar's wife tried to sleep with him, he didn't try to reason with her. He didn't stand there and pray about it. He ran. He left his coat and got out. Sometimes, the only spiritual warfare you need to do is use your legs and get out of the situation.

But the biggest lesson is forgiveness. You might be holding a grudge right now against a friend who stabbed you in the back. You think holding onto that anger protects you. It doesn't. It's like drinking poison and expecting the other person to die. Joseph forgave not because his brothers deserved it, but because he trusted God's justice more than his own revenge.

MESSIANIC THREAD Joseph was the beloved son, sent by his father to check on his brothers. His brothers rejected him, sold him for silver, and threw him into a pit. He was raised up to the right hand of the king and became the savior of the world, offering bread to the hungry. Does that sound familiar? It's the story of Jesus.

REFLECT

You meant it for evil, but God meant it for good. Write about a painful experience in your past that you can now see brought about something good or made you stronger.

....

....

....

Is there someone you need to forgive? Remember, forgiving others is proof that the love of God is working in you.. Write their name down and write, "I release you."

....

....

....

Joseph ran from temptation. What is a situation or a person you need to physically distance yourself from to keep your heart clean?

....

....

....

MICROHABIT

❒ Look at the one area of your life you hate right now (a boring class, a part-time job, chores). This week, do that task with 100% excellence, not for the teacher or your boss, but as an act of worship to God.

MY AFFIRMATION

Father, I thank You that You are the Master Strategist of my life. I reject the spirit of a victim; I am a victor in Christ Jesus. I declare that my current challenges are merely the training ground for my future. I refuse to be bitter. I choose to be better. I have the spirit of excellence, and I will bloom where I am planted. What the enemy meant for evil, You have already turned for my good. Hallelujah!

Get More

Genesis 37, 39, 45, 50:20

CHAPTER 6

Potiphar's Wife

NO PEACE ELSEWHERE

> *Guard your heart above all else, for it determines the course of your life.*
>
> **Proverbs 4:23 NLT**

She walked through the marble halls of the finest house in Egypt. She had servants to brush her hair, gold bracelets climbing up her arms, and a husband who was the captain of the Pharaoh's guard. She had everything a woman could want.

Except she was bored. And she was empty.

She watched the young Hebrew slave, Joseph. He was different. He didn't have her wealth, but he had a light in his eyes that she didn't possess. He was handsome, yes, but it was his integrity that intrigued and annoyed her. She wanted to own that. She wanted to consume it.

Lust is not love. Love gives; lust takes. She didn't care about Joseph's future, his God, or his soul. She only cared about what he could do for her in the moment to numb her boredom.

"Lie with me," she demanded.

It was an order from a woman used to getting her way.

But Joseph said no.

She was stunned. Rejection hit her like a slap in the face. How dare he? She was the mistress of the house! She wasn't used to boundaries. She wasn't used to hearing that her desires weren't the most important thing in the universe.

Day after day she pressed him. She tried to wear him down. This was the danger of discontentment. She had a husband, she had wealth, but she fixated on the one thing she couldn't have.

One day, she cornered him. She grabbed his garment. She was going to force him to validate her. But Joseph pulled away so hard he left his cloak in her hand and ran.

Standing there, holding the empty fabric, her desire curdled into something dark. If she couldn't have him, she would destroy him.

She cried out. She crafted a lie so perfect, so poisonous, that it would ruin him. "The Hebrew servant came in to mock me!" she cried.

She used her power to play the victim. She used a lie to try and crush an innocent man. Joseph was thrown into the dungeon, and she sat back in her palace, justified in her own eyes. But as she sat there, surrounded by her gold and her servants, she remained exactly what she was before: empty.

THE DOWNLOAD

We don't know her name, but we know her type. Potiphar's wife is the ultimate warning label for discontentment. You can have all the stuff (the clothes, the followers, the money) and still be miserable if your heart isn't right with God.

She teaches us a critical lesson about boundaries and authority. In our culture, we often feel we have a "right" to get what we want, whether that is a specific friendship, a leadership role, or recognition. But just because you desire something does not mean you are entitled to it.

We must also address the issue of rejection. When you are denied an opportunity, or when someone sets a boundary with you, it could sting. But Potiphar's wife demonstrates that rejection is never an excuse for revenge. You do not have the right to destroy the reputation of someone simply because they did not give you what you wanted.

The destructiveness of lies is grim here. Her gossip destroyed Joseph's physical freedom for years. Your words have power. In high school, a rumor is like a forest fire: easy to start, impossible to stop.

MESSIANIC THREAD Potiphar's wife falsely accused Joseph, leading to his condemnation. Centuries later, false witnesses would accuse Jesus, leading to His crucifixion. Joseph suffered for a sin he didn't commit; Jesus suffered for our sins, which He didn't commit, so that we could be free.

REFLECT

Have you ever wanted something just because you couldn't have it? Why do you think we do that?

....

....

....

How do you handle rejection? Do you get sad, or do you get mad and want to get even?

....

....

....

Lust takes, Love gives. Apply this to your current view of relationships. Are you looking for what someone can give you (status, comfort), or how you can serve them?

....

....

....

MICROHABIT

- ❐ This week, pay attention to how you talk about people who have annoyed you or rejected you. Are you spinning the story to make yourself look like the victim? Are you exaggerating their faults? Challenge yourself to speak strictly the truth, or say nothing at all.

MY AFFIRMATION

Father, I thank You that You are my portion and my satisfaction. I do not look to people or status to fill my soul. I am complete in Christ. I reject the spirit of entitlement; I do not need to manipulate others to feel powerful. I possess a heart of integrity and a tongue that speaks only the truth. I guard my heart with diligence, refusing to let bitterness or envy take root. Hallelujah!

Get More

Genesis 39:1-20

CHAPTER 7

Jochebed

STAND STRONG IN GOD

> *Trust in the Lord with all your heart, And lean not on your own understanding; In all your ways acknowledge Him, And He shall direct your paths.*
>
> ***Proverbs 3:5-6***

The sound of heavy sandals crunching on gravel was enough to stop Jochebed's heart. Every mother in Goshen knew that sound. It was the rhythm of death. It meant Pharaoh's soldiers were patrolling, hunting for the cry of a newborn boy to silence.

Inside the small, mud-brick home, the air was thick with humidity and terror. Jochebed looked down at the bundle in her arms. He was three months old now. He was getting bigger, his lungs were getting stronger, and his coos were turning into distinct cries that could pierce through the thin walls of their house. For ninety days, she had played a dangerous game of hide-and-seek with the most powerful empire on earth. She had hushed him, nursed him in the dark, and prayed over every whimper.

But she knew the time had come. She could no longer hide him. The logic of the world and the law of the King said her son was already dead. It would be easier to just give up, to let despair take over. But

Jochebed felt a fierce, burning resolve in her chest that defied the logic of her circumstances. She feared the sharp edge of Pharaoh's sword, yes, but she feared the God of Abraham more. And she trusted Him more.

"Miriam," she whispered, her voice steady despite the trembling of her hands. "Bring the reeds."

She didn't collapse in a heap of tears. Instead, she went to work. This was creativity in crisis. She sat on the dirt floor, her fingers moving with desperate precision. She took the papyrus reeds, plants that grew by the very river that was supposed to be her son's grave, and she began to weave.

It was beyond a basket. It was an ark of salvation.

She worked the materials until her fingers were raw. Then came the tar and the pitch. The smell was pungent, stinging her eyes, but she didn't stop. She daubed the sticky black substance over every inch of the weave, sealing it, waterproofing it, making sure that not a single drop of the Nile could get in. It was a practical, messy, sticky act of faith. She was engineering a miracle with her own hands.

When the sun began to dip, casting long shadows over the water, the basket was ready.

The walk to the riverbank felt like walking to her own execution. The Nile was wide and indifferent. Crocodiles lurked in the shallows. The current was unpredictable. Every instinct in her body screamed, *Keep him! Hold him! Don't let go!*

She kissed the boy's forehead, inhaling the scent of milk and baby skin one last time. She placed him into the basket. He looked so small against the dark pitch.

This was the moment of surrender. It wasn't enough to build the basket; she had to release it. She had to trust that the invisible hands of God were stronger than the currents of the river. With a prayer that had no words, just a groan of the soul, she pushed the basket into the reeds.

She watched it bob in the water. She didn't turn away, but she didn't interfere. She had done her part; the rest was God's.

She sent her daughter, Miriam, to watch from a distance. Jochebed went back to her empty house, the silence deafening. She waited. Minutes stretched into hours. Every rustle of the wind sounded like a soldier's footsteps.

Then, the door burst open. Miriam stood there, breathless, her chest heaving.

"Mother, come! Quickly!" she gasped, grabbing Jochebed's hand. "The Princess found him. She needs a nurse. I told her I knew someone."

Jochebed didn't ask questions. She didn't hesitate. She ran.

They reached the riverbank, lungs burning. The scene was surreal: Egyptian royalty standing amidst the mud and reeds, holding the crying Hebrew infant. The Princess looked at Jochebed, a slave woman with dust on her hem, with a gaze that wasn't hostile, but commanded authority.

"Take this child away and nurse him for me," the Princess commanded, her voice cutting through the humid air. "I will give you your wages."

Jochebed reached out, her hands trembling as she took her own son back into her arms. The weight of him was the same, but the reality had changed.

The God of the impossible hadn't just saved her son; He had manipulated the heart of the enemy to protect him. She would walk back into her home not as a fugitive hiding a secret, but as a hired nurse, paid by the King's own treasury to raise the deliverer of God's people.

THE DOWNLOAD

This story is every control freak's worst nightmare and greatest lesson. Jochebed had to put the thing she loved most into a river full of crocodiles.

We all have a "baby" we are trying to hide and protect with our own strength. Maybe it is a friendship you are trying to force, a grade you are obsessing over, or a reputation you are terrified of losing. We believe that if we white-knuckle our grip on these things, we can keep them safe. But Jochebed teaches us that surrender is actually a strategy. When she released control, God activated His plan.

Jochebed is also a masterclass in faith over fear of authority. She respected the King, but she didn't worship him. When the world tells you to do something that goes against God (whether it's the government, your school administration, or social pressure), you have a higher allegiance.

And how cool is the basket moment? Creativity in crisis. Sometimes we think faith means just sitting around praying. But Jochebed got to work. She used her hands. She engineered a solution. God used her practical skills to save Moses.

Here is the irony that only God can write: God pays your calling. Pharaoh tried to kill the babies, and ended up paying for Moses' daycare. When you take a risk for God, He provides for you in ways that don't make logical sense.

MESSIANIC THREAD Jochebed placed her son in an ark to save him from death in the water. Centuries later, God sent His Son, Jesus, to pass through the waters of death and rise again so that we could be safe in Him. Moses was the deliverer drawn from the water; Jesus is the Deliverer who gives living water.

REFLECT

What is the basket you are trying to weave right now? Is there a problem you need to solve with creativity and prayer?

....

....

....

Jochebed had to trust God with her son in a dangerous river. What is the scariest thing God is asking you to trust Him with right now?

....

....

....

Faith over fear. Describe a time you felt pressure from a teacher, boss, or group leader to do something that felt wrong. How did you handle it?

....

....

....

MICROHABIT

❐ Find a physical object that represents something you are worried about (a coin for money, a friendship bracelet for a relationship, a pen for grades). Go to a quiet place, hold it open-handed before God, and say, "I am not the owner of this; I am just the manager. I trust You with the outcome."

MY AFFIRMATION

Father, I thank You that You are the Sovereign Protector of my life and my future. I refuse to partner with the spirit of fear or anxiety. I possess the courage of Jochebed to trust You when the current is strong. I walk in divine strategy, supernatural peace, and absolute trust. Hallelujah!

Get More

Exodus 2:1-10

CHAPTER 8

Rahab

GETTING INTO THE HALL OF FAITH

> *By faith the harlot Rahab did not perish with those who did not believe, when she had received the spies with peace.*
>
> **Hebrews 11:31**

Jericho was a fortress, a city of stone and war, but for Rahab, it was a prison of reputation. She lived on the wall, literally. Her apartment was built into the city's massive defensive barrier. But the walls couldn't keep out the whispers.

Rahab the Harlot.

That was her name. That was her identity. When she walked to the market, heads turned, and then quickly turned away. She saw the judgment in the eyes of the other women, the "good" women who didn't sell their bodies to survive. She felt the weight of the label every single day. She was used goods. She was a mistake. She was on the outside of respectable society, looking in.

But lately, the whispers in the market weren't about her. They were about a people group moving through the desert like a swarm of locusts. The Israelites. They said their God, Yahweh, had split a sea in half. They said He had crushed the mighty kings of the Amorites.

Rahab looked at the stone idols in her room, silent, cold, dusty. Then she looked out her window toward the desert. A strange fear began to rise in her, but it wasn't just terror; it was awe. She knew, with a chilling certainty, that her city was doomed. The stone walls of Jericho felt flimsy compared to the stories of this God.

Then came the knock.

It wasn't a customer. It was two men, dusty, eyes darting nervously. Israelite spies.

In that split second, Rahab had a choice. She could scream. She could call the guards. She could be the hero of Jericho, the patriot who turned in the enemy. It would be the safe thing to do. It would be the logical thing to do.

But Rahab looked at them and saw something else. She saw a chance to defect. She saw a chance to be on the side of the God who split seas.

"Hide," she hissed, ushering them up to the flat roof, burying them under piles of drying flax stalks. The scratchy plants covered them completely.

Moments later, the King's soldiers hammered on her door. "Bring out the men who came to you!"

Rahab stood in the doorway. Her heart hammered against her ribs. This was treason. If they searched the roof, she would be executed before sunset.

"True," she lied, her voice steady, playing the part of the dim-witted woman they expected her to be. "The men came to me, but I didn't know where they were from. And when the gate was about to close at dark, the men went out. Pursue them quickly, for you will overtake them."

The soldiers bought it. They ran off into the night.

Rahab climbed back to the roof. She pulled back the flax and looked the spies in the eye. She didn't ask for money. She didn't ask for safety for herself alone.

"I know that the Lord has given you the land," she whispered, her voice trembling with a confession of faith that shamed the high priests of her city. "For the Lord your God, He is God in heaven above and on earth beneath."

She made them swear. Salvation for the family. She demanded that her father, mother, brothers, and sisters be spared.

"Bind this scarlet cord in the window," the spies told her. "When we come, everyone inside this house will live."

Days later, the ground shook. The trumpets blasted. The walls of Jericho, the massive, impenetrable stone, crumbled into dust. All of them.

Except for one section.

Standing amidst the rubble, like a lighthouse in a storm, was one small house with a red rope hanging from the window. Rahab stood there, her family huddled around her, watching the dust settle. The woman with the worst reputation in town was the only one left standing.

THE DOWNLOAD

Rahab's story is the ultimate clapback to cancel culture. In her city, she was trash. She was defined by her sin and her profession. Labels don't define you. People called her "Harlot," but God called her "Saved." In fact, when the New Testament was written, this foreign prostitute was listed in the "Hall of Faith" alongside heavyweights like Moses and Abraham.

Rahab teaches us that faith requires risk. It wasn't safe to hide those spies. She put her neck on the line. Sometimes, following God means going against your culture, your school, or even your family's expectations. She chose protecting God's people over protecting her own comfort.

And look at her heart for her family. She didn't just want to save herself; she negotiated salvation for the family. Her faith became an umbrella that protected everyone under her roof.

But the most powerful image is the scarlet cord. The spies told her to hang a red rope from her window. That red rope was the only thing that stopped the judgment of God from hitting her house. It is a direct picture of the blood of Jesus. It doesn't matter what Rahab had done the night before. It didn't matter what her reputation was. As long as she was behind the red cord, she was safe.

MESSIANIC THREAD Rahab didn't just survive; she married an Israelite prince. She became the great-great-grandmother of King David. And do you know who is in her direct family tree? Jesus. The King of Kings chose a former outcast for His own family tree. That means there is no past too dark for God to use in His future.

REFLECT

What is a label you are afraid will stick to you forever?

....

....

....

Rahab took a huge risk for a God she barely knew. What is one risk you feel God is calling you to take?

....

....

....

Who in your family or friend group needs you to pray for their salvation, like Rahab fought for her family?

....

....

....

MICROHABIT

- ❒ Write down the negative labels people have put on you (or you have put on yourself) on a piece of paper. Take a red marker and write REDEEMED in big letters over them. Rip the paper up and throw it away.

MY PRAYER

Precious Father, thank You that Your grace is stronger than my history and that the blood of Jesus covers every mistake. I am so grateful that You do not define me by the labels of the world, but by Your redeeming love. Because I am safe in You, I have the courage to step out in faith and trust You with my future. Amen.

Get More

Joshua 2:1-21, Joshua 6:22-25

CHAPTER 9

Deborah

THE MOTHER WHO WENT TO WAR

> *The LORD is my light and my salvation; Whom shall I fear? The LORD is the strength of my life; Of whom shall I be afraid?*
>
> **Psalm 27:1**

The air under the palm tree was thick with heat and the sound of arguments.

"He stole my sheep!" one man shouted.

"He moved the boundary stone!" the other yelled back.

Deborah rubbed her temples. She sat on her usual stone seat in the hill country of Ephraim. She wasn't a queen in a silk robe; she was a judge in the dust. People came to her from all over Israel because they knew one thing: when Deborah spoke, she gave God's word.

She looked at the men, her eyes sharp but kind. With a few sentences, she cut through their excuses and settled the dispute. They left quietly, humbled by her authority.

But today, the disputes over sheep felt trivial. There was a shadow over the land. The cruel King Jabin and his commander, Sisera, had 900 iron chariots. Israel had nothing but farm tools and fear. For twenty years, the people had been crushed.

Deborah paused her judgments. She turned to a messenger. "Summon Barak from Kedesh in Naphtali," she ordered. When he arrived, the commander of Israel's army looked tired. He looked like a man who had done the math and knew he was going to lose.

"The Lord commands you," Deborah said, her voice shifting from counselor to commander. "Go, take with you ten thousand men to Mount Tabor. God will give Sisera into your hands."

Barak hesitated. He looked at the woman sitting under the palm tree.

"If you go with me, I will go," Barak said, his voice low. "But if you don't go with me, I won't go."

A silence hung between them. Deborah could have mocked him. She could have told him to man up. Instead, she stood. She smoothed her robes. She didn't belittle his fear; she simply lent him her faith.

"Very well," she said, her confidence absolute. "I will go with you."

She didn't need a sword. She had something sharper: a direct line to God. She knew what she had heard.

Fast forward to the battlefield. The ground shook as 900 iron chariots thundered toward them. It should have been a massacre. But Deborah wasn't looking at the chariots; she was looking at the sky.

"Up!" she cried to Barak. "This is the day the Lord has given Sisera into your hands."

And then, the impossible happened. The skies tore open. Rain, torrents of it, slammed into the earth. The dry ground turned into a swamp. The terrifying iron chariots stuck fast in the mud. The enemy panicked.

God had fought for them.

When the dust settled and the victory was won, Deborah didn't rush to the podium to take credit. She didn't start a lecture tour on "How I Beat the Bad Guys." She did what she always did. She gathered the people, and she sang.

Awake, awake, Deborah! Awake, awake, break out in a song!

She was a leader, a judge, and a warrior. But in her song, she gave herself a title that mattered more than all of those: *A Mother in Israel.*

THE DOWNLOAD

Deborah shatters our stereotypes of leadership. She was governing the nation and commanding generals.

But notice where her confidence came from. It wasn't "Self-Love" or "Girl Boss" energy. It was Godfidence. She could sit under that palm tree and give orders to generals because she had spent time listening to God's voice. She didn't need Barak to validate her. In fact, Barak needed her validation.

This story hits home because we often feel the pressure to shrink. Maybe you are naturally decisive, or you have a strong intellect, and you feel the temptation to "play small" so you don't intimidate your friend group or stand out too much in class. Deborah teaches us that leadership is stewardship. If God gave you a voice, you are responsible to use it.

But here is the key: she used her power to empower, not to destroy. When Barak was scared, she didn't cancel him. She went with him. She was a mother to her community. You don't have to have kids to be a mother. Being a mother in the spiritual sense means you nurture the people around you. You protect them. You help them grow.

MESSIANIC THREAD Deborah was a judge who delivered her people from oppression, bringing 40 years of peace. Jesus is the ultimate Judge who delivers us from the oppression of sin, bringing us eternal peace. Deborah fought a battle involving a tree and a river; Jesus won the ultimate battle on a tree (the cross) so that rivers of living water could flow through us.

REFLECT

Deborah was confident because she heard God clearly. What distracts you the most from hearing God's voice (e.g., social media, busyness, worry)?

....

....

....

Have you ever dumbed down your intelligence or leadership skills to make someone else feel comfortable? How did that make you feel?

....

....

....

Deborah called herself a "Mother in Israel." Who is one person in your life that you can mother (nurture, guide, or protect) right now?

....

....

....

MICROHABIT

❒ Find someone this week who is struggling or lacks confidence (a friend nervous about a presentation, a sibling trying out for a team). Instead of just saying "good luck," be a Deborah. Say, "I believe in you, and I'm going to help you." Then, actually help them prepare or show up to cheer them on.

MY AFFIRMATION

Father, I thank You that You have not given me a spirit of fear, but of power, love, and a sound mind. I possess the wisdom of Christ to navigate every challenge. I do not shrink back in the face of intimidation; I stand tall in my God-given calling. As I walk out my purpose today, I bring strength into those around me. Hallelujah!

Get More

Judges 4:1-16, Judges 5:1-7

CHAPTER 10

Gideon

THE MAJORITY IS WITH GOD

> *But God has chosen the foolish things of the world to put to shame the wise, and God has chosen the weak things of the world to put to shame the things which are mighty.*
>
> ***1 Corinthians 1:27***

The air in the winepress was choked with dust and chaff. It was a hole in the ground, really, a place meant for crushing grapes, not for threshing wheat. But Gideon didn't care about proper farming techniques. He cared about survival.

He beat the wheat stalks furiously, glancing up at the rim of the pit every few seconds. He was terrified. For seven years, the Midianites had swarmed over the land like locusts, stealing crops, burning villages, and killing anyone who resisted. They were a massive, unstoppable army. And Gideon? Gideon was a nobody. He was the youngest son of the weakest family in the smallest tribe.

He was hiding. That was his strategy. Stay low, stay quiet, stay alive.

"The Lord is with you, you mighty man of valor!"

Gideon spun around, his heart leaping into his throat. A Man was sitting under the terebinth tree, watching him. The Stranger's voice was calm, but the words felt like a cruel joke.

Mighty man of valor? Gideon looked down at his dusty clothes and his shaking hands. He was hiding in a hole.

"Pardon me, my lord," Gideon replied, the sarcasm and bitterness spilling out. "If the Lord is with us, why has all this happened to us? Where are all His miracles our fathers told us about? The Lord has forsaken us."

The Lord (for it was Him) didn't strike Gideon down for his doubt. He simply looked at him with a gaze that saw the future, not the present. "Go in this might of yours, and you shall save Israel from the hand of the Midianites. Have I not sent you?"

Gideon laughed, a nervous, incredulous sound. Your limitations are not an excuse, but Gideon had plenty of them. "Me? My clan is the weakest in Manasseh, and I am the least in my father's house."

But God wasn't looking for a resume. He was looking for a vessel.

Even after the call, Gideon struggled. He was anxious. He was an overthinker. He asked God for signs, once with a fleece of wool being wet while the ground was dry, and then again with the fleece dry and the ground wet. He needed reassurance. It is okay to ask God questions. God, in His infinite patience, answered every single one.

Finally, the day of battle came. Gideon had gathered 32,000 men. It felt like enough to maybe, just maybe, hold the line.

"Too many," God said.

Gideon blinked. "Excuse me?"

"The people are too many. If you win now, you'll think you did it yourselves."

God whittled the army down. He sent home the fearful 22,000. Then He tested them by how they drank water from the stream. In the end, Gideon stood looking at his army.

300 men.

300 men with trumpets and clay jars against a Midianite army of 135,000 that covered the valley like sand.

It was a suicide mission. But Gideon had learned something in the winepress. He had built an altar called *Jehovah Shalom*, The Lord is Peace. He realized that peace is a person, not a circumstance.

That night, at God's command, the 300 men surrounded the enemy camp. They didn't draw swords. They smashed their clay jars, revealing burning torches, and blew their trumpets.

"For the Lord and for Gideon!"

The sudden light and noise in the pitch black sent the Midianites into a panic. In the confusion, they turned their swords on each other. Gideon watched as the Lord threw the enemy into chaos, sparking the victory. But Gideon was no longer hiding; the man who once cowered in a winepress now led the pursuit as the liberator of his nation.

THE DOWNLOAD

Gideon is the prime example for anyone who has ever felt unqualified. We resonate with this story because Gideon is so transparent. He isn't brave like David or strong like Samson. He is sarcastic, unsure, and hesitant.

God defines you by your potential, not your present. When God saw Gideon, He didn't see a coward in a winepress; He saw a general in the making. God calls things that are not as though they were. You might feel like the quiet girl or the average student, but God sees the spiritual giant inside you.

Gideon tried to use the "I'm not enough" card. Your limitations are not an excuse. In fact, God prefers your limitations because they make His power look even better.

And the army math? Small numbers can make a big impact. We are obsessed with numbers, likes, followers, squad size. God isn't. He cut the army from 32,000 to 300 to prove that one girl plus God is a majority. You don't need a huge platform to change the world; you just need obedience.

I love that Gideon asked about the fleece. It is okay to ask God questions. God isn't fragile. He can handle your doubts. Gideon wasn't doubting God's power; he was doubting his own worthiness. God met him right there.

MESSIANIC THREAD Gideon won the victory not by military strength, but by breaking clay vessels to let the light shine out. Decades later, Paul writes in 2 Corinthians that "we have this treasure in earthen vessels, that the excellence of the power may be of God and not of us." Gideon's broken jars point to us. We were once a broken people, now we are shining the light of Jesus into a dark world.

REFLECT

Gideon called himself the least of the least. How do you describe yourself to yourself?

....

....

....

What is a fleece you need to put out? Is there a decision you are anxious about where you need to ask God for clarity?

....

....

....

Jehovah Shalom. How can you find peace this week in the middle of a stressful situation (exams, drama, family issues)?

....

....

....

MICROHABIT

- ❒ The next time you are about to do something you're unsure about (send a risky text, buy something you can't afford, join in on a mean joke), physically stop. Count to five. Ask yourself: "Does this look good, or is it actually good?"

MY AFFIRMATION

Father, I thank You that You have called me by a name that is greater than my past or my feelings. I am a mighty girl of valor, chosen and commissioned by You. I refuse to hide in the shadows of insecurity. I break the jars of limitation today, and I let Your light shine through me in my home and my school. Hallelujah!

Get More

Judges 6:11-40, Judges 7:1-22

CHAPTER 11

Delilah

SILVER OVER SOUL

> *Faithful are the wounds of a friend, But the kisses of an enemy are deceitful.*
>
> **Proverbs 27:6**

"Eleven hundred shekels of silver. From each of us."

The number hung in the cool night air of the Valley of Sorek, heavy and intoxicating. Delilah sat on her divan, her fingers tracing the rim of a wine goblet. She looked at the Philistine lords standing in the shadows of her room. They were powerful, dangerous men, but right now, they looked desperate.

She did the math quickly. Five lords. Eleven hundred pieces of silver each. That was five thousand five hundred shekels. It was a fortune. It was enough to buy a palace, an army, and a new life. It was enough to buy her soul.

"And all you have to do," one of the lords hissed, "is find out where his great strength lies."

Samson. The brute with the long hair and the short temper. The man who tore lions apart with his bare hands and slaughtered Philistines for sport. He was infatuated with her. She knew it. She saw the way his eyes glazed over when she walked into the room. He was physically invincible, but emotionally? He was a child.

"Consider it done," she whispered, a small, cold smile playing on her lips.

When the lords left, the transaction was sealed. It wasn't about love; it was about leverage.

Later, when Samson arrived, filling the doorway with his massive frame, Delilah didn't see a lover. She saw a paycheck. She welcomed him with open arms, the scent of jasmine and myrrh masking the stench of her betrayal.

"Tell me, please," she cooed, running her fingers through the thick, matted locks of his hair. "What makes you so strong? How could someone tie you up and subdue you?"

He lied to her, of course. First, he said fresh bowstrings. Then new ropes. Then weaving his hair into a loom. Each time, she sprang the trap. "The Philistines are upon you, Samson!" And each time, he snapped the bonds like charred thread, laughing at the ambush.

But Delilah didn't give up. She knew the power of toxic influence. She knew that water, dripping constantly on a stone, will eventually crack it. She didn't fight him with muscles; she fought him with nagging. She weaponized her emotions.

"How can you say, 'I love you,' when your heart is not with me?" she cried, turning her face away, summoning fake tears. "You have mocked me three times."

Day after day, she pressed him. She made his life miserable. She poked at his insecurity. She questioned his love. She created an atmosphere so suffocating that he felt he had no room to breathe. The Bible says "his soul was vexed to death." She broke him with her words.

Finally, he cracked. He couldn't handle the pressure anymore. He told her everything. The Nazirite vow. The razor. The hair.

Delilah stopped crying instantly. Her eyes dried. She knew this was the truth.

She called the lords. She took the cold, heavy silver, before she even finished the job. Greed had won her heart.

She waited until he was asleep, his head heavy on her lap, the lap that should have been a place of safety, not a slaughterhouse. She signaled the barber. She watched as the seven locks of hair fell to the floor, silent and soft.

She felt his strength leave him. It was a tangible shift in the room, like a candle being blown out.

"The Philistines are upon you, Samson!" she shouted one last time.

He woke up, thinking, *I will go out as before.* But he didn't know the Lord had left him. The Philistines seized him. They gouged out his eyes.

Delilah stood back, clutching her bag of silver. She had won the fortune, but she had lost her humanity. She watched the man who loved her being dragged away to a life of grinding darkness. She clutched her bag of silver tighter. She had won the fortune, but she had sold her soul to get it.

THE DOWNLOAD

Delilah is the original toxic girlfriend. We see her and think, *I would never do that.* But let's look closer.

Delilah fell into the trap of greed. She valued things more than people. In our world, this looks like using people for what they can give you, rides, popularity, connections, rather than loving them for who they are. If you are friends with someone just because of their status, you have a little bit of Delilah in your heart.

She also mastered the misuse of charm. She used her beauty and her emotions to manipulate. Have you ever given someone the silent treatment to get your way? Have you ever cried just to make someone feel guilty? That is manipulation, and it is destructive. Be the girl who builds a man up, not the one who nags him until he breaks. Your influence should be a shelter, not a storm.

For us, there is also a warning to identify your weaknesses. Samson fell because he couldn't say "no" to her. He compromised his values because he wanted to please a girl. We must recognize who influences us negatively. If you have a friend who constantly drags you down or pressures you to sin, that is a similar spirit to Delilah. Run.

Betrayal leaves a mark. Delilah got her money, but history remembers her as a monster. Trust is expensive; don't trade it for cheap thrills.

MESSIANIC THREAD Delilah betrayed Samson, the judge of Israel, for pieces of silver. In the New Testament, Judas betrayed Jesus for 30 pieces of silver. Samson was bound and blinded; Jesus was bound and blindfolded. But here is the difference: Samson died taking revenge on his enemies; Jesus died forgiving His enemies.

REFLECT

Have you ever used guilt or emotion to get someone to do what you wanted? How did it affect the relationship?

....

....

....

She valued silver more than love. What is something (popularity, grades, money) that you are tempted to value more than your relationships?

....

....

....

Who is the Samson in your life (someone you influence greatly)? Are you building them up or tearing them down?

....

....

....

MICROHABIT

- [ ] Scroll through your Close Friends list or your recent texts. Is there anyone you are manipulating? Or is there anyone who makes you feel "vexed to death" or pressured to compromise your standards? Unfollow, mute, or have a brave conversation to set a boundary.

MY PRAYER

Dear Heavenly Father, thank You for the spirit of discernment and the heart of integrity You have placed within me. I rejoice that I am Your child, defined by Your truth rather than the approval of others or the lure of temporary gain. I walk in wisdom today, building genuine relationships that honor You and guarding the relationship I have with You. Amen.

Get More

Judges 16:4-21

CHAPTER 12

Hannah

THE POWER OF A VOW

> *Call upon Me in the day of trouble; I will deliver you, and you shall glorify Me.*
>
> **Psalm 50:15**

The feast at Shiloh was loud. There was the smell of roasted meat, the sound of laughter, and the clinking of cups. Families were celebrating. But Hannah sat alone in the corner, her plate full but untouched. Her throat felt tight, like a fist was squeezing it.

Across the room, Peninnah was glowing. Peninnah, her husband's other wife, had a lap full of children. She had sons pulling at her robe and daughters braiding her hair. And she made sure Hannah saw it.

"Still nothing, Hannah?" Peninnah's voice was sweet poison. "Maybe next year. Or maybe God just doesn't favor you."

The words cut deep. This was handling bullying 101. Peninnah provoked her severely to make her irritable. She poked at the deepest wound in Hannah's soul: her empty womb. In a culture where a woman's value was tied to having sons, Hannah felt forgotten.

Her husband, Elkanah, tried to help. "Am I not better to you than ten sons?" he asked. He loved her, but he didn't understand. His love couldn't fix the ache of unfulfilled purpose.

Hannah couldn't take it anymore. She stood up. She didn't scream at Peninnah. She didn't flip the table. She went to the house of the Lord.

She fell to her knees in the dust. She was weeping so hard her body shook, but no sound came out. She was pouring out her soul.

"O Lord of hosts," she moved her lips silently, "if You will indeed look on the affliction of Your maidservant and remember me... I will give him to the Lord all the days of his life."

It was a desperate, raw bargain. She wasn't asking for a baby to show off to Peninnah. She was asking for a son to give back to God.

Eli, the priest, was watching her. He saw a woman trembling, lips moving, eyes red. He thought the worst.

"How long will you be drunk?" he scolded her. "Put your wine away from you!"

Even the priest misunderstood her pain. Hannah looked up, tears streaming down her face. "No, my lord... I am a woman of sorrowful spirit. I have poured out my soul before the Lord."

Eli paused. He saw the truth in her eyes. "Go in peace," he said, softening. "And the God of Israel grant your petition which you have asked of Him."

And then, the miracle happened. Not the pregnancy that came later. The miracle was the shift in Hannah. The Bible says she went her way and ate, and "her face was no longer downcast."

She hadn't held a baby yet. Her circumstances hadn't changed. But she had changed. She had transferred the burden from her shoulders to God's.

A year later, the silence in Hannah's house was broken by a cry. She named him Samuel, "Because I asked the Lord for him."

And when the boy was weaned, perhaps three years old, Hannah did the hardest thing imaginable. She packed his bag. She took him to Shiloh. She walked up to Eli. Keeping promises is agonizing when it costs you your heart, but she did it.

"For this child I prayed," she said, her voice trembling with pride and grief. "Therefore I also have dedicated him to the Lord."

She left her only son at the tabernacle. She walked away empty-handed, but full-hearted, knowing that prayer changes things.

But that wasn't the end of Hannah's song. You cannot out-give God. As the years passed, the Lord visited Hannah again. Her womb, once a source of shame, became a testimony of abundance. The Bible records that she conceived and bore three more sons and two daughters. The woman who once sat alone in the corner became a joyful mother of many, proving that when you surrender your best to God, He restores it with interest.

THE DOWNLOAD

Hannah's story is a hug for anyone struggling with their mental health. The Bible doesn't hide her depression. She wept. She couldn't eat. She was bitter of soul.

This teaches us that It is okay to weep, grieve, and be emotional in God's presence. God doesn't want your fake "I'm fine" prayers. He wants your ugly cry. He wants your raw honesty.

Hannah also shows us how to deal with a Peninnah. We all have someone who knows exactly how to push our buttons. Hannah didn't seek revenge. She took her pain to the only One who could actually solve it.

The most powerful moment is the mental health change. Notice that she felt better after she prayed, but before she was pregnant. Prayer isn't a vending machine where you put in a coin and get a prize. Prayer is an exchange. You give God your worry; He gives you His peace.

Hannah made a vow in the dark, and she kept it in the light. Keeping promises to God is rare today. Because she gave Samuel back to God, Samuel became the prophet who anointed King David.

MESSIANIC THREAD Hannah dedicated her firstborn, Samuel, to the Lord's service, and afterwards, she was blessed with many more children. This mirrors the story of the Gospel. God the Father gave up His only begotten Son, Jesus, for our salvation. Because Jesus was planted as a seed, He became the firstborn among many brethren (Romans 8:29). God gave one Son, and in return, He reaped a harvest of children all over the world, including you.

REFLECT

What is a bitter emotion you have been bottling up? Write a raw, unfiltered letter to God about it.

Is there a promise you made to God or a friend that you haven't kept? How can you make it right?

How do you usually react to people who tease or bully you? How can Hannah's example change that?

MICROHABIT

- ❒ When you feel overwhelmed, close your eyes. Imagine you are holding a heavy basket labeled with your problem. Imagine Jesus standing in front of you with His hands out. Physically make the motion of handing the basket to Him. Take a deep breath and say, "It's Yours now."

MY PRAYER

Heavenly Father, I thank You that I have direct access to Your presence. Thank You that I am not a victim of my circumstances, but a victor in Christ Jesus. I acknowledge that You are the Source of my joy and the answer to every petition. I stand firm in the knowledge that You are faithful to Your word, and I choose to be faithful to mine. I trade my heaviness for Your garment of praise, walking in confidence that Your will is being established in my life. Amen.

Get More

1 Samuel 1:1-28

CHAPTER 13

Jonathan

LOYALTY ABOVE AMBITION

A friend loves at all times, and a brother is born for adversity.

Proverbs 17:17

The spear whistled past Jonathan's ear, missing him by inches, and slammed into the stone wall behind him. The vibration of the wood hummed in the shocked silence of the feast hall.

Jonathan did not sit frozen in fear. He stood up in fierce anger, refusing to eat, grieving not just for David, but for his father's shame. The King's face was twisted, purple with a rage that had become all too familiar lately. The royal dinner table, usually a place of strategy and laughter, had become a minefield. And the target of this rage? David.

"You son of a perverse, rebellious woman!" Saul screamed, his voice echoing off the pillars. "Do I not know that you have chosen the son of Jesse to your own shame? For as long as the son of Jesse lives on the earth, you shall not be established, nor your kingdom!"

Jonathan, with his heart pounding, left the table without a word, the truth settling heavy in his gut. His father was right about one thing: As long as David lived, Jonathan would never be king. By all the laws of succession, the throne belonged to Jonathan. David was the threat. David was the rival.

But Jonathan didn't see a rival. He saw a brother.

He walked out into the cool night air, his mind racing back to the day they met. David had just killed Goliath, standing there holding a giant's head, dusty and bloody. In that moment, Jonathan had felt something shift in the spiritual atmosphere. He recognized the anointing of God on the shepherd boy.

Most princes would have killed the competition. Jonathan did the unthinkable. He had taken off his royal robe, the symbol of his rank, his future, his very identity, and draped it over David's shoulders. He gave him his sword, his bow, and his belt. It was a silent surrender. *You are the one God has chosen, not me.* Selfless friendship meant giving up his rights to honor God's choice.

Now, the toxicity in the palace was suffocating. Jonathan loved his father, but he could not support his father's sin. Navigating toxic family dynamics was a daily war. How do you honor a parent who is actively doing evil? Jonathan realized he had to draw a line. He could respect the King's position, but he would not participate in the King's madness.

The next morning, Jonathan went to the field. He shot the arrows, the secret signal he and David had agreed upon.

"The arrow is beyond you!" Jonathan shouted to his servant, his voice cracking.

David emerged from his hiding place in the rocks. He looked tired. He looked hunted. They fell into each other's arms, weeping. It wasn't a casual "see ya later." It was a grieving of what could have been.

"Go in peace," Jonathan whispered, gripping David's shoulders. "We have sworn friendship in the name of the Lord."

Jonathan watched David walk away into the wilderness. He knew he might never see him again. But years later, when David was hiding in the woods of Ziph, terrified and exhausted, Jonathan would find him one last time. He wouldn't go to bring him back to the palace. He wouldn't go to switch sides. He would go for one purpose: to strengthen his hand in God.

Jonathan returned to the palace to face his father's wrath alone, keeping his covenant to the end. He chose loyalty over royalty.

THE DOWNLOAD

We throw the word "friend" around loosely. A friend is someone who likes your TikToks or sits with you at lunch. But Jonathan redefines the word. He shows us what a covenant friend looks like.

Jonathan had every reason to hate David. David was taking his job! Peer and family pressure told him to cut David off. But Jonathan chose loyalty over peer pressure. He realized that his loyalty to God's plan was more important than his loyalty to his father's ego.

This is tricky, right? Navigating toxic family dynamics is one of the hardest things a teenager can face. Maybe your parents push you to be popular, or dislike your Christian friends, or acts in ways that embarrass you. Jonathan teaches us that you can honor your parents without agreeing with their sin. You can love them while still standing up for what is right.

And look at the lack of jealousy. Jonathan gave David his robe. He was basically saying, "You're going to be the main character, and I'm okay with being the supporting cast." Selfless friendship is cheering for your friend when they get the scholarship, or the lead role you wanted.

Jonathan's superpower was encouragement. When he visited David in the woods, he didn't bring money or weapons. He strengthened his hand in God. He reminded David of God's promises when David had forgotten them.

MESSIANIC THREAD Jonathan was the son of the King who stripped himself of his royal robe and humbled himself so that David could be lifted up. Jesus is the Son of the King who stripped Himself of His heavenly glory and humbled Himself so that we could be lifted up and made co-heirs with Him.

REFLECT

Is there a relationship in your life where you feel jealous of the other person's success? Confess that to God today.

....

....

....

How do you handle it when your parents or family members want you to do something that goes against your conscience?

....

....

....

Jonathan was a safe place for David. Who is a safe place for you? Who are you a safe place for?

....

....

....

MICROHABIT

❒ Scroll through your contacts and find a friend who is going through a time of stress, sadness, or loneliness. Send them a text right now that isn't just "thinking of you," but actually reminds them of a specific promise of God.

MY PRAYER

Father, thank You that You have given me a secure place in Your Kingdom. I thank You that I do not need to fight for position or recognition, for You are the One who promotes. I appreciate the friends You have placed in my life, and I thank You for the strength to be a loyal "Jonathan" to them. I walk in the spirit of unity, honoring Your choice in others and serving Your purpose with a humble heart. In Jesus' Name. Amen.

Get More

1 Samuel 18:1-4, 1 Samuel 19:1-7, 1 Samuel 20, 1 Samuel 23:16-18

CHAPTER 14

The Widow of Zarephath

SACRIFICE REQUIRES FAITH

> *And my God shall supply all your need according to His riches in glory by Christ Jesus.*
>
> ***Philippians 4:19***

The heat in Zarephath was physical. It pressed down on the cracked earth like a heavy blanket. There had been no rain for years. The ground was gray, the sky was brass, and the silence of the town was the silence of slow death.

The woman moved slowly, her feet dragging in the dust. Her stomach had stopped rumbling days ago; now it was just a hollow ache. She scanned the ground for sticks. Two sticks. That was all she needed. Just enough to build a tiny fire.

She wasn't planning a dinner; she was planning a funeral.

She had a handful of flour left in the bottom of the jar. Maybe a few drops of oil in the jug. She would mix them, bake a small cake for herself and her son, they would eat it, and then they would lie down and wait to die. That was the plan. It was grim, but it was certain.

"Please, bring me a little water in a cup."

The voice startled her. A man was standing near the city gate. He looked rough, dusty, wearing a garment of hair. An Israelite.

She hesitated. Water was gold right now. But she nodded. As she turned to go, he added the request that broke her heart.

"Please bring me a morsel of bread in your hand."

She stopped. She turned back, her eyes filling with hot tears. The audacity.

"As the Lord your God lives," she said, her voice trembling, "I do not have bread. Only a handful of flour in a bin, and a little oil in a jar. I am gathering two sticks to make it for myself and my son, that we may eat it and die."

There. She said it. She was empty. She had nothing to give.

The man, Elijah, looked at her. He didn't apologize. He didn't offer her money. He said the most impossible thing: "Do not fear... make me a small cake from it first, and bring it to me; and afterward make some for yourself and your son."

First? Give him the last bit? Trusting God with your last can be terrifying. It goes against every survival instinct. But there was something in his voice. He didn't just give his word; he gave God's Word. "For thus says the Lord God of Israel: The bin of flour shall not be used up until the rain came."

She looked at the sticks in her hand. She looked at her starving son. She looked at the prophet.

She made the choice. She went home. She scraped the bottom of the jar. She poured the last drop. She baked the bread and gave it away.

And then, she went back to the jar.

There was flour in it. Not a lot. Not a full sack. Just enough for the next meal.

Day after day, for months, it was the same miracle. She would scrape the jar empty, go to sleep, and wake up to find just enough for that day. Daily provision. She never got a warehouse full of food; she got a daily promise.

But the test wasn't over. Later, her son, the one she had kept alive, fell sick. His breathing stopped. The grief was immediate and violent. Handling disappointment with God is messy. She turned on Elijah immediately. "What have I to do with you, O man of God? Did you come to remind me of my sin and kill my son?"

She thought God was punishing her. She thought the miracle was a setup.

But Elijah didn't scold her. He took the boy to the upper room. He cried out to God. And God, who crosses borders and defies death, put breath back into the boy's lungs.

THE DOWNLOAD

This story makes zero sense mathematically. You cannot subtract from zero and get a positive number. But God's math is different.

The widow teaches us about giving when you feel empty. We often think, "I'll be generous when I have more." When I have more money, more time, or more energy. But this woman gave when she was at rock bottom. Generosity is a posture of the heart, not the size of your bank account.

She also learned about daily provision. We want the 5-Year Plan. We want to see the full scholarship, the future husband, the guaranteed career. God usually gives us just enough light for the step we are on. The flour didn't overflow; it just didn't run out. God gives you strength for today.

Notice something huge: God crosses borders for you. Jesus brings this woman up in Luke 4. He points out that there were many widows in Israel, but Elijah was sent to a Gentile in Zarephath (enemy territory). This means God will cross social, cultural, and physical lines to find you. You are never too far out for God.

And when her son died, she blamed herself. "Did you come to remind me of my sin?" We do this too. Something goes wrong, and we think, "God is punishing me for that thing I did last summer." That is not how grace works. God isn't keeping a list of your sins to use against you later. He is in the business of resurrection, not revenge.

MESSIANIC THREAD This widow gave her only son's last meal to the prophet. Later, God gave His only Son to become the Bread of Life for us. She gave bread and received life; we receive the Bread of Life and live forever.

REFLECT

What is something you feel empty of right now (patience, hope, money, energy)?

....

....

....

God gives enough for today. Does that stress you out or comfort you? Why?

....

....

....

Have you ever felt like God was punishing you when something bad happened? Write about that honestly.

....

....

MICROHABIT

- [ ] When you get your allowance or paycheck next, give 10% (tithe) to your local church. Before you buy the coffee, before you save. Give God the first of what you have, even if it's small, as an act of trust that He will handle the rest.

MY AFFIRMATION

I live by the economy of the Kingdom of God, not the economy of this world. I do not fear lack, for the Lord is my Shepherd. I am generous, joyful, and prompt to obey the voice of God. My security is not in my savings, my job, or my connections, but in the Word of the Lord that cannot fail. Hallelujah!

Get More

1 Kings 17:7-24, Luke 4:25-26

CHAPTER 15

Elijah

STRENGTH IN THE STILLNESS

> *Be still, and know that I am God.*
>
> **Psalm 46:10**

Elijah was running. His chest heaved, his legs burned, and sweat stung his eyes. He was running away from a threat.

Just 24 hours ago, he had been on top of the world. On Mount Carmel, he had called down fire from heaven. He had defeated 450 prophets of Baal. He had prayed down rain after a three-year drought. He was the ultimate spiritual superhero.

Then came the message from Queen Jezebel: *By this time tomorrow, I will make your life like one of them.* Meaning: You're dead.

Panic seized him. The adrenaline crash was brutal. He ran into the wilderness, far away from anyone, and collapsed under a broom tree. The silence of the desert amplified the noise in his head.

"It is enough!" he groaned, curling into a ball in the dirt. "Now, Lord, take my life, for I am no better than my fathers!"

This was the great prophet of God, and he was suicidal. He was exhausted, terrified, and feeling like a total failure. Comparison kills your spirit, and Elijah was comparing himself to the prophets of old and feeling like he didn't measure up.

He closed his eyes, hoping not to wake up.

But God didn't send a lightning bolt to zap him for his lack of faith.

An angel touched him gently. "Arise and eat."

There, on hot stones, was a fresh cake of bread and a jar of water. Elijah ate. He drank. And then he went back to sleep.

God knew what Elijah needed. Physical self-care is a spiritual act. He didn't need a rebuke; he needed a snack and a nap.

After he rested, he traveled to a cave on Mount Horeb. He sat in the darkness, feeling sorry for himself. The word of the Lord came to him, asking, 'What are you doing here, Elijah?' Elijah replied, 'I have been very zealous for the Lord," he complained. "I alone am left, and they seek to take my life."

Loneliness distorts your reality. Elijah truly believed he was the only believer left on the planet. The isolation made the problem feel infinite.

Then, God told him to stand on the mountain.

A great wind tore into the mountains, shattering rocks. But the Lord was not in the wind.

An earthquake shook the ground. But the Lord was not in the earthquake.

A fire raged. But the Lord was not in the fire.

Then, a sound. A still, small voice. A gentle whisper.

Elijah wrapped his face in his mantle. God speaks in the whisper. He wasn't in the big, dramatic, noisy events. He was in the quiet intimacy.

In that whisper, God gave Elijah a reality check. "I have reserved seven thousand in Israel who have not bowed to Baal." *You are not alone, Elijah. You're just tired.*

And then, God gave him the cure for his isolation: purpose. "Go," God commanded. He didn't just send him to find a friend; He sent him to shape history. "Anoint Hazael as king over Syria, Jehu as king over Israel, and Elisha... to be prophet in your place." God showed Elijah that his work wasn't done; he still had a future. And in Elisha, God gave him a partner to pour into so he wouldn't have to carry the heavy burden alone.

THE DOWNLOAD

Elijah's experience on Mount Horeb is not just a story about being tired; it is a lesson on spiritual stamina and the deception of isolation. Elijah had just won a massive public victory, but the enemy attacked him in the quiet aftermath.

First, understand the principle of divine sustenance. The angel provided supernatural nourishment that sustained Elijah for forty days and nights. Your body is the temple of the Holy Spirit. Maintaining your physical vessel through rest and nutrition is an act of stewardship that enables you to carry the weight of your spiritual assignment. You cannot drive a car with no fuel; do not expect to run your race without rest.

Watch out for the lie of loneliness. Loneliness distorts your reality. When you are sad, your brain tells you, "No one likes me. I'm the only Christian at this school. No one understands." That is a lie. God had to remind Elijah that there were 7,000 others. You have sisters in faith, even if you can't see them right now.

We have to learn to turn down the volume. We live in a world of earthquakes and fires, constant notifications, drama, breaking news. But God speaks in the whisper. You have to get quiet to hear Him.

God cured Elijah by giving him a steward in Elisha. When you are depressed, you want to isolate. That is the worst thing you can do. Force yourself to connect. Find a mentor, or become a mentor. Shared burdens are lighter.

MESSIANIC THREAD Elijah was a prophet who performed miracles, fasted for 40 days, and ascended to heaven. He points to Jesus, the ultimate Prophet, who fasted 40 days, performed miracles, and ascended to heaven. But while Elijah felt alone, Jesus was truly left alone on the cross so that we would never have to be forsaken.

REFLECT

I am no better than my ancestors. In what areas are you comparing yourself to others and feeling like a failure?

....

....

....

Rate your physical self-care this week on a scale of 1-10. How is it affecting your mood?

....

....

....

Who is your Elisha? Who is someone you can reach out to for connection or to help them growing?

....

....

....

MICROHABIT

- ❐ This week, pick one hour (maybe before bed) to put your phone on airplane mode or in another room. No music, no podcasts, no scrolling. Just silence. Sit in it. Let your brain decompress so you can hear the whisper. You can do this with your Bible whilst meditating on scripture.

MY AFFIRMATION

I am part of the faithful remnant of God. I am not alone, and I am not abandoned. The joy of the Lord is my strength, and His peace guards my mind. I have the discipline to silence the noise of the world and tune into the still, small voice of the Holy Spirit. My body is a temple, and I steward it with wisdom and rest. I refuse to agree with the lies of discouragement; I agree with the assignment God has placed on my life. I am strengthened for the journey! Hallelujah!

Get More

1 Kings 19:1-18

CHAPTER 16

The Shunammite Woman

BEING SECURE

> *Now godliness with contentment is great gain.*
>
> ***1 Timothy 6:6***

The sun in Shunem was unrelenting, baking the limestone walls of the house until they radiated heat. But the woman standing on her roof wasn't thinking about the temperature. She was thinking about the man who passed by her house every few weeks.

Elisha. The holy man.

She watched him walk down the dusty road, humble, weary, yet carrying an atmosphere of authority that made the hair on her arms stand up.

Discernment is a gift to those who pay attention. She perceived a spiritual weight. She recognized the anointing because she was watching for it." Her radar was pinging loud and clear. *This man is holy. We need to bring him into our orbit.*

"Let us make a small upper room on the wall," she told her husband that night. "Let us put a bed for him there, and a table and a chair and a lampstand."

She was wealthy. She could have used her money to buy new jewelry, expand her own quarters, or throw lavish parties to impress the neighbors. Instead, she was using what she had to build a sanctuary for God's work.

One day, Elisha, resting in the cool, quiet room she had built, sent his servant Gehazi to her. He was grateful. He wanted to repay her.

"What can be done for you?" Gehazi asked. "Do you want me to speak to the King or the commander of the army for you?"

Imagine that. A blank check. A direct line to the President. Access to the highest levels of power and fame. Most people would have jumped at the chance for a glow up, a promotion, or a favor to cash in later.

The woman smiled, a smile of profound peace. "I dwell among my own people."

Translation: *I'm good. I don't need the King to know my name to feel important. I don't need a platform. I am content right here, serving where my feet are planted.*

But her story didn't end in that quiet room. Years later, the miracle son Elisha had prophesied for her was in the field. He grabbed his head, screaming in pain, and died in his mother's arms.

Panic should have set in. Screaming. Hysteria. But the Shunammite woman possessed a terrifyingly beautiful resilience. She carried the boy's body up to the prophet's room and laid him on the bed. She shut the door.

She ordered a donkey. "Run," she told her servant. "Do not slow down unless I tell you."

When she saw Elisha in the distance, he sent Gehazi to ask, "Is it well with you? Is it well with the child?"

"It is well," she said.

It wasn't a lie; it was a declaration of faith. She refused to agree with death. She refused to panic. She knew that if she could just get to the source of the power, the situation could be reversed.

When she reached Elisha, she fell at his feet. She refused to be brushed aside. She refused to leave. Persistence was her weapon now. "As the Lord lives, and as your soul lives, I will not leave you."

She didn't leave until he got up. She marched the prophet back to her house, back to that upper room, and waited while he prayed. And because she knew who she was, because she used what she had, and because she refused to give up, she received her son back alive.

THE DOWNLOAD

In a world of pick-mes, where everyone is desperate to be noticed, verified, or invited to the VIP section, the Shunammite woman is worth emulating.

When offered a favor from the King, she basically said, "No thanks, I'm happy with my crew." That is contentment on a soul level. She didn't need external validation or "upgrades" to feel worthy. She was secure in her identity. If you are constantly chasing the next trend, or the popular group to feel good about yourself, you are building your house on sand.

She also teaches us about discernment. She perceived that Elisha was holy and made room for him. We must be discerning about who we invite into our private worlds. Not everyone deserves access to your heart, your thoughts, or your time. Protect your upper room.

Finally, consider her response to crisis: "It is well." This is the language of faith. Resilience isn't denying the reality of the problem (her son was dead!); it is denying the problem the right to destroy your confession. She refused to speak death. She maintained her confession of faith until she reached the source of power. She didn't panic; she went to the place of prayer.

MESSIANIC THREAD This woman built a room for the prophet, and in that room, her son was raised from the dead. We prepare room for Jesus in our hearts, and He raises us from spiritual death. Also, her son died and was raised back to life, a foreshadowing of the death and resurrection of Christ.

REFLECT

I dwell among my own people. Do you feel the need to be popular, or are you content with the friends God has given you?

....

....

....

Describe a time you had discernment about a person or situation. Did you listen to it?

....

....

....

If God offered you anything right now, would you ask for something worldly or something spiritual?

....

....

....

MICROHABIT

❒ Look at your bedroom. Is it a place where peace can dwell, or is it chaotic? This week, clean your room. Dedicate a specific chair or corner as your upper room, somewhere you only do peaceful things (read, pray, journal), no scrolling allowed.

MY AFFIRMATION

I am secure in who God created me to be. I do not crave the applause of people or the validation of the culture. I am content in my assignment, and I steward my influence with wisdom and grace. I have the spirit of discernment; I recognize what is holy and I make room for it in my life. When challenges arise, I hold fast to my confession. My words align with God's report, not the world's report. All is well with my soul, my mind, and my future! Hallelujah!

Get More

2 Kings 4:8-37

CHAPTER 17

Daniel

THE RESOLUTION OF THE HEART

> *But Daniel purposed in his heart that he would not defile himself with the portion of the king's delicacies.*
> ***Daniel 1:8***

The smell was incredible. Roast meats, rich gravies, wines imported from the finest vineyards. The king's table in Babylon was a feast for the senses. For a group of teenage boys who had been ripped away from their destroyed homes in Jerusalem, this food was real temptation to forget who they were.

Daniel looked at the spread. He knew the meat had been sacrificed to idols. He knew the wine was part of pagan rituals. To eat it was to agree with the system. It was to say, "I am a Babylonian now."

Most of the other captives shrugged and ate. *Why make a scene?* they thought. *We are slaves. We have to survive.*

But Daniel had made a decision long before he smelled the food. Conviction starts small. He had resolved in his heart that he would not defile himself.

He spoke to the chief official, who was afraid. So Daniel turned to the steward appointed over them. He didn't flip the table. He didn't start a protest or scream about how evil Babylon was. He used respectful dissent.

"Please," Daniel said, "test your servants for ten days. Give us vegetables to eat and water to drink."

He was polite, but he was immovable. He was resisting peer pressure on a massive scale. He was risking his head, but he trusted his God.

Ten days later, Daniel and his friends looked better, healthier, and sharper than the boys eating the king's steak. Excellence acts as a shield. Because they were disciplined, they stood out.

Fast forward. Daniel is now an old man, a high-ranking official. He has survived kings and coups. But his enemies are jealous. They want to take him down. They dig through his emails, his files, his history. They are looking for dirt, corruption, a bribe, a lie.

They find nothing.

He was so excellent at his job that they couldn't find a single fault. The only way to trap him was to use his faith against him. They tricked the King into signing a law: *No praying to anyone but the King for 30 days.*

Daniel heard the law. He knew the penalty: The Lion's Den.

He didn't hide. He didn't close his windows. He didn't pray silently in his head. He went to his upper room, opened his windows toward Jerusalem, and knelt down. Three times a day. Just as he had done yesterday. Just as he would do tomorrow.

Consistency.

He did it because prayer was his lifeline.

They threw him to the lions. The beasts circled him, hungry, smelling blood. But the God who honors those who honor Him sent an angel to shut their mouths.

Daniel spent the night in a pit of death as if it were a VIP lounge.

When the stone was rolled away the next morning, Daniel was unscratched. He had stood alone, and because of that, the entire empire learned who the true God was.

THE DOWNLOAD

Daniel is the ultimate prototype of how to live in a Babylon world without becoming a Babylonian. You are surrounded by a culture that wants you to eat its food, consume its media, adopt its values, sleep around, party, and forget God.

Daniel teaches us that conviction starts small. You can't wait until you are in the backseat of a car with a boy to decide your sexual boundaries. You can't wait until the cheat sheet is passed around to decide if you are honest. You have to decide now. Daniel purposed in his heart before the plate was ever set in front of him.

He also mastered respectful dissent. A lot of Christians are known for what they hate. We get angry, we judge, we yell. Daniel showed respect to the guard. You can stand up for your beliefs without being a jerk.

And look at the power of excellence. Daniel was so good at his job that his haters came up empty. If you are a Christian, you should be the best student, the most hardworking employee, the most reliable teammate. Your excellence protects your witness.

Finally, consistency. Daniel didn't pray because he was in a crisis; he was in a crisis and kept praying because it was his habit. His routine sustained his faith. If you only pray when things go wrong, you won't have the strength to stand when the lions come.

MESSIANIC THREAD Daniel was innocent, yet condemned to a pit of death. A stone was rolled over the mouth of the pit. But God brought him out alive. Jesus was the Innocent One, condemned to the pit of death (the tomb). A stone was rolled over the entrance. But God raised Him to life, defeating the roaring lion (Satan) forever.

REFLECT

What is a line in the sand you need to draw right now? A decision you need to make before the pressure comes?

....

....

....

They could find no corruption in him. If someone dug through your phone and private messages right now, what would they find?

....

....

....

Are you consistent in your time with God, or only when you need something?

....

....

....

MICROHABIT

- ❒ Pick one "King's Food" item in your life (social media, a specific Netflix show, negative music, or junk food) and give it up for 10 days. Replace it with something spiritual (prayer, reading, worship music). See if you don't feel "healthier and sharper" at the end.

MY AFFIRMATION

I have an excellent spirit within me. I am in this world, but I am not of it. I possess the wisdom of God to navigate complex situations with integrity and honor. I have purposed in my heart to walk in holiness, and I do not compromise my standards for temporary approval. My habits of prayer and the Word are consistent, building a fortress of faith that stands in the day of trouble. I am distinguished by the Spirit of God! Hallelujah!

Get More

Daniel 1, Daniel 6

CHAPTER 18

Esther

POSITIONED FOR PURPOSE

> *For God has not given us a spirit of fear, but of power and of love and of a sound mind.*
>
> ***2 Timothy 1:7***

"Three days without food makes the gold weigh heavier on your head."

Esther stared at her reflection in the polished bronze mirror, but she didn't recognize the girl looking back. The kohl lining her eyes was perfect. The silks draped over her frame were worth more than her cousin Mordecai would earn in a lifetime. She looked like a queen. She looked like the perfection of Persian nobility. But beneath the layers of myrrh and expensive dye, her heart was hammering against her ribs like a trapped bird.

Do not imagine that you in the king's palace can escape any more than all the Jews.

Mordecai's message had hit her like a physical blow earlier that week. Until then, the palace had been a cage, yes, but a gilded one. It was safe. It was comfortable. It was silent. Now, the silence was screaming. Outside these walls, Haman's decree was already etched in wax: her people were going to be annihilated.

She touched her neck. If she walked into the inner court without being summoned, the King's guards had orders to strike her down. One step, and her head could roll across the marble floor.

"Hathach," she whispered to her attendant, her voice trembling. "Is it time?"

The eunuch nodded solemnly. "The King is seated."

Esther closed her eyes. For a year, she had been prepped for beauty. She had been soaked in oils, scrubbed, perfumed, and taught to walk in a way that pleased the eye. The world and the King valued her for her face. They thought her power lay in her beauty. But as she stood up, steadying herself on the vanity, Esther realized that her beauty was just the key that unlocked the door. It wasn't the weapon.

Her weapon was the fasting. Her weapon was the three days she and her handmaidens had spent prostrate on the floor, weeping before the God of Israel, stripping away the vanity of the palace until only raw faith remained.

She took a breath. It felt like inhaling jagged glass. *If I perish, I perish.*

She began the long walk down the corridor. The guards at the heavy cedar doors stiffened. They didn't know she was a Jew; they only knew she was breaking the law. As the doors groaned open, the light from the throne room blinded her momentarily.

There sat King Xerxes. Immense. Terrifying. A man who had deposed his last wife for a single act of public defiance.

Every instinct in Esther's body screamed at her to run. To go back to her room, hide behind her perfumes, and hope the slaughter passed her by. But she remembered Mordecai's question: *Who knows whether you have not come to the kingdom for such a time as this?*

She wasn't just a pretty girl in a palace. She was a placement. She was a strategy of God, positioned behind enemy lines before the war even began.

Esther locked her knees to stop them from shaking. She lifted her chin, not with arrogance, but with the dignity of a daughter of God. She stepped into the line of sight.

The room went silent. The King turned. His eyes narrowed.

Time seemed to suspend. This was the moment. The collision of a death sentence and divine purpose. And then, slowly, miraculously, the King extended the golden scepter.

She lived. And because she lived, a nation would survive.

THE DOWNLOAD

We live in a world that is obsessed with the glow up. We scroll through TikTok and Instagram, bombarded by the message that our value is tied to our aesthetic. If we just had the right skin routine, the right body, or the right clothes, then we'd be "queens."

But look at Esther. History remembers her, but not because she had great hair or perfect skin. There were hundreds of other beautiful women in that harem. Esther is remembered because when the pressure was on, she realized that her position wasn't for her pleasure, but for purpose.

We often think that God blesses us just so we can be happy. But what if God gave you that influence, that spot on the cheer team, that academic gift, or that specific group of friends because He needs an agent on the inside?

Esther teaches us a tough lesson about advocacy. She had strategic privilege. She was safe in the palace. She could have stayed silent and survived. But she realized that privilege is a weapon to be used to protect those who are vulnerable. If you have a voice, status, or stability that others do not, you are responsible for using it.

Courage is not the absence of fear; it is the mastery of it. Esther was terrified. But she moved anyway. She understood that she was a divine strategy positioned behind enemy lines.

MESSIANIC THREAD Esther risked her life to go before an earthly king to save her people from physical death. Centuries later, Jesus gave His life to go before the Heavenly King to save us from eternal death. Esther needed the King to extend a golden scepter of grace so she could live. Because of Jesus, God extends the scepter of grace to us every single day. We can approach the throne of grace boldly, not because we are worthy, but because we are His.

REFLECT

For such a time as this. Do you feel like you are in your current school, family, or friend group by accident, or do you believe God placed you there? Why?

Esther had to risk her reputation and safety. What is one thing you are afraid of losing if you were to stand up for your faith or for others?

In what areas of your life are you focusing more on "outer beauty" (preparation of the body) than "inner strength" (preparation of the spirit)?

MICROHABIT

- [ ] This week, identify one person in your circle who is usually overlooked or being treated unfairly. Be an Esther to them. You don't have to make a grand speech. Just sit with them at lunch, talk to them in the hallway, or shut down gossip when you hear it. Use your social capital to spend it on someone who needs it.

MY PRAYER

Father, I thank You that You have orchestrated my life and placed me exactly where I am. I thank You that I am not just a face in the crowd, but a daughter of the King with a specific assignment. I embrace my identity as a woman of influence and courage. I declare that I will not remain silent when You call me to speak. I walk in the confidence that Your favor surrounds me like a shield. In Jesus' Name. Amen.

Get More

Esther 4:10-16, Esther 5:1-3, I recommend you read the whole book.

CHAPTER 19

Mary

THE BRAVE YES

> *Then Mary said, "Behold the maidservant of the Lord! Let it be to me according to your word." And the angel departed from her.*
>
> **Luke 1:38**

The whisper was barely a breath in the dark, but it shattered her world.

"Greetings, O favored one, the Lord is with you!"

Mary froze. She was from Nazareth, a dusty, forgettable town where nothing important ever happened. She was engaged to Joseph, a good man, a carpenter. Her life was mapped out: a quiet wedding, a small house, children, and obscurity.

But the angel Gabriel stood before her, radiating a light that made the oil lamp in the corner look like a dying ember. He spoke of a baby. A King. The Son of the Most High.

"How will this be?" she asked, her voice trembling. Not "No," but "How?"

The answer was terrifying. The Holy Spirit would overshadow her. She would carry the Messiah.

Mary's mind raced. She knew the law. She knew the culture. To be pregnant and unmarried was social suicide. It was a scandal. At best, Joseph would divorce her quietly. At worst, she could be stoned to death. Her reputation would be shredded. The whispers would follow her for the rest of her life. *That girl. The one who got in trouble.*

She stood on the precipice of the unknown. She didn't understand the biology. She didn't understand the politics. She certainly didn't understand the pain that lay ahead. But she looked into the light and made a choice. She chose to surrender to the unknown.

"Behold the maidservant of the Lord! Let it be to me according to your word."

She said "Yes" to the risk. She was trusting God with her reputation, believing that His promise was worth her shame.

Fast forward. The angel was gone. The glory faded. Now came the reality. The mundane. The season in Egypt running from Herod. The years in Nazareth washing tunics, baking bread, sweeping dust.

It wasn't always miracles and angels. Most of it was faithfulness in the mundane. It was raising a toddler who was also her God. It was wiping the nose of the Savior of the world. It was quiet obedience when no one was watching.

Mary didn't broadcast her experiences. When the shepherds came with wild stories, or when Simeon prophesied in the temple, she didn't post it for attention. The Bible says she "kept all these things and pondered them in her heart." She understood the value of pondering things in her heart. She was a deep thinker, holding the mystery of God in a private, sacred space.

But the "Yes" she whispered in Nazareth led her to a hill she never wanted to climb. Golgotha.

She stood at the foot of the cross. Most of the disciples had fled in terror. But Mary stayed. She watched the boy she had nursed, the man she had raised, hang in agony. A sword pierced her own soul, just as Simeon had predicted.

She didn't scream. She didn't collapse. She stood. This was endurance through pain. In the face of absolute heartbreak, she maintained a dignity and a strength that defied human logic. She was there for His first breath, and she was there for His last. Her "Yes" had cost her everything, but as she looked up at Him, she knew, even through the tears, that He was purchasing something far greater than her comfort. He was purchasing life.

THE DOWNLOAD

Mary is often depicted on Christmas cards as serene and passive, but her life reveals a warrior spirit. Being chosen by God did not make her life simple; it made it dangerous. Her story challenges us to redefine the concept of surrender.

We like to say "Yes" to God when the plan includes a scholarship, a promotion, or a win. But what about when the plan includes confusion? Mary said "Yes" without seeing the script. She trusted the Director.

She also hits us hard on reputation. In high school, your reputation is your currency. The fear of being "canceled" or looked down on is paralyzed. Mary risked being the town outcast to carry Jesus. Are you willing to look weird or uncool for your faith?

I love that she was a thinker. Pondering is a lost art. We process everything externally now, on stories, in group chats, in captions. Mary teaches us that some spiritual moments are just for you and God. Keep some secrets with Him. It builds intimacy.

Notice also that Mary was a thinker. The Bible says she "pondered these things in her heart." We live in an era of external processing: posting, sharing, and broadcasting every thought. Mary teaches us the discipline of the inner life. Some spiritual treasures are meant to be kept between you and God. Intimacy is built in the secret place, not the public square.

Finally, consider her endurance. Mary's "Yes" eventually led her to the foot of the cross. She watched her Son die, yet she did not collapse in hysteria. She stood. She modeled a dignity that refuses to be crushed by pain. She understood that the pain of the moment was purchasing an eternal weight of glory.

MESSIANIC THREAD Mary gave physical birth to the Body of Christ (Jesus). Later, through His death and resurrection, Jesus gave spiritual birth to the Body of Christ (the Church). Mary labored in pain to bring Him into the world; He labored in pain on the cross to bring us into the Kingdom.

REFLECT

Let it be to me according to your word. What is one area of your life where you are struggling to say "Yes" to God because you are afraid of the outcome?

....

....

....

Mary risked her reputation. Are you hiding your faith to protect your social status? Be honest.

....

....

....

How do you handle mundane seasons where nothing exciting is happening? Do you check out, or do you stay faithful?

....

....

....

MICROHABIT

- [ ] Identify one boring or repetitive task you usually complain about (folding laundry, math homework, emptying the dishwasher). Before you start, stop and say, "I am doing this as unto the Lord." Do it with excellence and without grumbling. Remind yourself that you aren't just doing a chore; you are practicing the same faithfulness Mary showed during her quiet years in Nazareth.

MY AFFIRMATION

I am a servant of the Most High God. I live in a state of active surrender, declaring "Yes" to the plans of God before I even know what they are. I am not ruled by the fear of man or the need for reputation; my identity is secure in Christ. I have the strength to carry heavy assignments and the patience to be faithful in the mundane. Hallelujah!

Get More

Luke 1:26-38, Luke 2:19, John 19:25-27

CHAPTER 20

Martha

BE STILL IN THE LORD'S PRESENCE

But seek first the kingdom of God and His righteousness, and all these things shall be added to you.

Matthew 6:33

The kitchen was a war zone. Pots were boiling over, the smell of roasting lamb filled the air, and Martha was sweating. This wasn't just any dinner. Jesus was here. The Messiah was in her home.

Martha was the hostess, the responsible one, the Type A older sister who made sure everything ran perfectly. She chopped, she stirred, she wiped. She wanted everything to be excellent for Jesus because she loved Him. This was her love language: Service.

But as she frantically arranged the bread platter, she glanced into the other room. There sat her sister, Mary. Just sitting. Sitting at Jesus' feet, listening to Him talk, completely oblivious to the chaos in the kitchen.

Resentment bubbled up in Martha's chest, hotter than the stew on the fire. *Does she not care? Does she think this food cooks itself?*

Martha snapped. She marched into the room, wiping her hands on her apron, her face flushed with frustration. She interrupted the Son of God.

"Lord, do You not care that my sister has left me to serve alone? Therefore tell her to help me!"

It was an accusation. *Lord, if You cared, You wouldn't let me work this hard.*

Jesus looked at her. He didn't scold her for working; He loved her heart to serve. But He saw the anxiety vibrating off her.

"Martha, Martha," He said, saying her name twice with gentle affection. "You are worried and troubled about many things. But one thing is needed, and Mary has chosen that good part, which will not be taken away from her."

He called her out on her priorities. Service vs. Presence. It is good to serve, but not at the expense of connection. Martha was so busy working for Jesus that she was missing Jesus.

Months later, the dynamic shifted. The kitchen was cold. The house was filled with weeping. Lazarus, their brother, was dead.

When Martha heard Jesus was finally coming (four days late!), she didn't wait in the house. She ran to meet Him on the road. And here, we see the raw beauty of Martha's heart: honesty in prayer.

She looked at the One she loved and said, "Lord, if You had been here, my brother would not have died."

She didn't sugarcoat her disappointment. She was heartbroken, and she told Him. But in the same breath, she showed a belief in the impossible. "But even now I know that whatever You ask of God, God will give You."

Jesus asked her, "Do you believe that I am the resurrection and the life?"

Martha, standing in the shadow of death, gave one of the greatest confessions in the Bible. "Yes, Lord, I believe that You are the Christ, the Son of God."

She believed before the miracle happened.

She went back and called Mary. She watched as Jesus commanded the stone to be rolled away. And she, the practical one, worried about the smell, "Lord, by this time there is a stench." But she stood by and watched as her brother walked out of the grave.

Martha was a woman of hospitality, opening her home to God. But she learned that the greatest hospitality is a heart that sits still enough to listen.

THE DOWNLOAD

If you are the girl who organizes the group projects, plans the parties, and stresses out when things aren't perfect, then you are a Martha. And that is a gift! The church needs Marthas.

But Martha teaches us a dangerous truth: You can be so busy doing "Christian things" (youth group, volunteering, leading worship) that you forget to actually spend time with Christ. Jesus defended Mary's choice to sit and listen. Why? because you can't pour from an empty cup.

Martha also teaches us about priorities. The worries of this life (grades, sports, drama) can easily choke out the "one thing needed." Jesus didn't say Martha's work was bad; He said it was distracting her from the best thing.

However, we must also honor Martha's fortitude. In John 11, she displays massive spiritual maturity. While standing in the face of death and disappointment, she confesses, "I believe that You are the Christ." She didn't wait for the resurrection to believe; she believed while her brother was still in the grave. That is the definition of faith.

MESSIANIC THREAD Martha worried about serving bread to Jesus. Jesus is the Bread of Life who was broken for us. Martha worried about her brother's physical death. Jesus came to defeat spiritual death so that "whoever lives and believes in Me shall never die."

REFLECT

Are you more of a Mary (presence) or a Martha (service)? What is the danger of your specific tendency?

....

....

....

You are worried and troubled about many things. List the top 3 things causing you anxiety right now. surrender them to the "One thing needed."

....

....

....

Have you ever felt like God showed up late (like with Lazarus)? Write a prayer being honest about that disappointment.

....

....

....

MICROHABIT

- ❐ For the next 3 days, set a timer for 5 minutes. Do not pray a list. Just sit in silence with God. If your mind wanders to your to-do list, gently bring it back to Jesus. Practice just being with Him without performing for Him.

MY PRAYER

Father, I thank You that I do not have to earn Your love through performance. Thank You that I am defined by who I am, not by what I do. I acknowledge that You are the Resurrection and the Life, and You hold my future in Your hands. I choose today to position myself at Your feet, receiving Your Word so that I may serve You with a peaceful heart. I declare that I am focused, settled, and secure in You. In Jesus' Name. Amen.

Get More

Luke 10:38-42, John 11:17-44

CHAPTER 21

The Samaritan Woman

YOU DON'T HAVE TO THIRST AGAIN

> *But whoever drinks of the water that I shall give him will never thirst. But the water that I shall give him will become in him a fountain of water springing up into everlasting life.*
>
> **John 4:14**

Noon. The sun was directly overhead, turning the dust of Samaria into a furnace. No one went to the well at noon. The respectable women went in the cool of the morning, laughing, talking, sharing news.

But she went at noon.

She went alone because she couldn't handle the side-eyes. She couldn't handle the whispers. *There she goes. Husband number five? Or is it six?*

She was tired. Tired of the heavy water jar. Tired of the heat. But mostly, tired of the empty ache in her chest that she kept trying to fill with men. Satisfaction always seemed just out of reach. Every relationship promised to fix her, and every relationship left her more broken than before.

She approached the well, eyes down. There was a man sitting there. A Jew. Her stomach tightened. Jews hated Samaritans. They treated them like dogs. She prepared for him to ignore her or spit on the ground.

"Give Me a drink," He said.

She stopped. He was talking to her? No social barriers. He was crossing racial lines, gender lines, and moral lines just by making eye contact.

"How is it that You, being a Jew, ask a drink from me, a Samaritan woman?" she deflected, her guard up.

Jesus looked at her. He didn't see a "loose woman." He saw a thirsty daughter. "If you knew the gift of God... you would have asked Him, and He would have given you living water."

Then, He dropped the bomb.

'Go, call your husband, and come here.'

She froze. The shame washed over her hot and fast. 'I have no husband,' she whispered, technically telling the truth.

'You have well said,' Jesus replied, His voice gentle but piercing. 'For you have had five husbands, and the one whom you now have is not your husband.'

He knew. He knew the messy, broken, scandalous history. Stunned, she stammered, 'Sir, I perceive that You are a prophet.' Desperate to shift the spotlight off her sin, she pivoted to theology. 'Our fathers worshiped on this mountain, and you Jews say that in Jerusalem is the place where one ought to worship.'

She tried to hide behind religious debate. But Jesus used her question to reveal the heart of the Father. 'God is Spirit, and those who worship Him must worship in spirit and truth.'

The realization hit her like a lightning bolt. This wasn't just a prophet. This was the Answer.

She looked at her water jar, the symbol of her daily burden, her constant thirst. She left it. She literally dropped it in the dirt. Her transformation into a witness was instant. She didn't care about the whispers anymore. She ran back to the town, the very people she had been avoiding.

"Come, see a Man who told me all things that I ever did!" she shouted. "Could this be the Christ?"

The woman who was too ashamed to be seen in the morning became the evangelist of the city by the afternoon. She found the Water that finally satisfied, and she couldn't keep it to herself.

THE DOWNLOAD

We all carry a "water jar." It is the external source we return to repeatedly, hoping it will define us, validate us, or make us feel whole. For the Samaritan woman, it was relationships. For others, it is academic status, social rank, or the dopamine hit of digital approval.

Jesus introduces the principle of superior satisfaction. Physical water (earthly validation) only solves the problem temporarily; you will always thirst again. But Jesus offers living water, a spiritual vitality that becomes a fountain inside of you. You do not need to look for satisfaction out there because you carry the source in here. When you are filled with the Spirit, you stop begging the world to make you happy.

Notice how Jesus handled the interaction. He dismantled social barriers not by ignoring the truth, but by speaking to the potential within her. He crossed racial, gender, and moral lines to find a worshiper. We are called to see people not for their reputation, but for their redemptive potential.

I love that she left her water jar. That jar represented her old life; her cycle of thirst and temporary filling. When she met Jesus, she abandoned her past burdens to run toward her future.

And she became a witness! Transformation into a witness doesn't require a theology degree. She just said, "Come see a guy who knows my mess and loves me anyway."

Finally, Jesus clarified the nature of worship. It is not about the location (the mountain or the temple); it is about the condition of the spirit. God is looking for those who worship in Spirit and truth. You can access the throne room of God in your classroom just as powerfully as in a sanctuary.

MESSIANIC THREAD She came to draw water from a well dug by Jacob. Jesus is the "Root of Jesse" (Jacob's line) who provides Living Water. She had had five husbands and was living with a sixth who wasn't her husband. Jesus came to be the Seventh Man in her life, the number of completion/perfection, the true Bridegroom of her soul.

REFLECT

What are the 5 husbands in your life: the five things you have tried to find satisfaction in that failed you?

....

....

....

He told me all things I ever did. Does the idea that Jesus knows everything about you scare you or comfort you? Why?

....

....

....

Who is someone outside your social circle that you can show kindness to this week?

....

....

....

MICROHABIT

❒ When you feel lonely or bored this week, pay attention to what you reach for first. Is it your phone? The fridge? A specific person? Stop and say, "This is just well water. Lord Jesus, You are the Living Water. You satisfy me."

MY PRAYER

Dear Father, I thank You that You are the Fount of Living Water. Thank You that I never have to thirst for validation or love, because I am overflowing with Your Spirit. I acknowledge that I am known fully by You and loved completely. I stand in the truth that You are my satisfaction. I walk today as a woman made whole. In Jesus' Name. Amen.

Get More

John 4:1-42

CHAPTER 22

The Woman with the Issue of Blood

FAITH THAT FIGHTS

> *Fight the good fight of faith, lay hold on eternal life, to which you were also called and have confessed the good confession in the presence of many witnesses.*
>
> ***1 Timothy 6:12***

"If they knew, they would kill me."

The thought looped in her mind, a rhythmic chant of terror that matched the pounding of her heart. She pulled her shawl tighter over her face, keeping her eyes fixed on the dusty ground. The noise of the crowd was deafening, shouts, laughter, the braying of donkeys, the shuffling of sandals. To anyone else, it was just a busy street in Capernaum. To her, it was a minefield.

For twelve years, she had been bleeding. Twelve years of weakness. Twelve years of doctors taking her money, offering bizarre remedies that only made the pain worse. But the physical pain was nothing compared to the social death. According to the Law, she was unclean. Anything she touched became unclean. Anyone she sat near became unclean.

She was a walking contagion. She hadn't felt the touch of a human hand, a hug, a handshake, in over a decade. She was a ghost in her own city, living in the shadows of shame.

But today, a rumor had pierced the darkness. *Jesus of Nazareth is passing by.*

She saw Him through a gap in the press of bodies. He looked ordinary, yet the air around Him seemed to vibrate with life. A desperate, wild hope flared in her chest. *If I can just touch His clothes,* she told herself, *I will be healed.*

She began to move. She had to push through the crowd. Elbows struck her ribs. Heavy feet stomped on her sandals. The smell of unwashed bodies and heat was suffocating. Her legs, weak from anemia, threatened to buckle. Every instinct screamed at her to turn back, to hide, to stay safe in her sickness.

But she kept pushing. She crawled. She shoved. She ignored the risk of being discovered and stoned.

She reached out. Her trembling fingers brushed the tassel of His prayer shawl.

ZAP.

Pure, raw, electric virtue, shot from the hem of His garment into her fingertips and flooded her body. The bleeding stopped instantly. The cold ache in her womb was replaced by a warmth she hadn't felt in years. She was whole.

She froze, tears welling in her eyes. *I did it. Now, run.*

"Who touched Me?"

The voice stopped the entire parade. The crowd hushed. Peter, the disciple, laughed nervously. "Master, the multitudes are thronging You and pressing You, and You say, 'Who touched Me?'"

Hundreds of people were bumping into Him. But Jesus knew the difference between an accidental bump and a desperate pull.

He looked around. His eyes found hers.

There was nowhere to hide. She was terrified. She fell face down in the dirt, trembling but truthful. She expected anger. She expected Him to shout, "Unclean!" She expected Him to cast her out for contaminating Him.

Instead, she poured out the whole story. The sickness. The poverty. The shame. The touch.

Jesus listened. He didn't recoil. He looked at the woman who had been an outcast for 4,380 days, and He gave her a new name.

"Daughter," He said. "Be of good cheer; your faith has made you well. Go in peace."

Daughter. Not woman. Not sinner. Not patient. Family. In one sentence, He healed her body and rewrote her identity.

THE DOWNLOAD

This story absolutely undoes me every time. For twelve years, this woman was defined by her condition. She was known simply as "The Bleeding Woman." You may feel defined by your own labels: "The Anxious One," "The Failure," or "The One Who Made That Mistake."

Jesus performed a radical identity shift. He took her label as an outcast and shredded it. He called her daughter. It is the only time in the recorded

Gospels that Jesus calls a woman by this specific, intimate title. He claimed her. He made her family.

But she had to fight for it. She had to push through the crowd. There will always be obstacles between you and Jesus. Sometimes the crowd is your friends who think church is lame. Sometimes the crowd is your own insecurity telling you you're too dirty to pray. You have to shove past that.

We also learn a crucial lesson: Faith vs. Proximity. Hundreds of people were touching Jesus that day. They were close to Him physically, but they didn't get healed. Why? Because they were just bumping into Him. Only she touched Him with faith. Going to youth group, listening to Christian music, or growing up in a Christian home puts you in proximity to Jesus. But proximity doesn't save you. You have to personally reach out and grab hold of Him.

Finally, she was trembling but truthful. She was scared to death to speak up, but she told the whole truth. There is freedom in reality. You do not have to perform for God. You can come to Him shaking, as long as you come to Him honest.

MESSIANIC THREAD According to Levitical law, if a bleeding person touches you, you become unclean. But when this woman touched Jesus, He didn't become unclean; she became clean. Jesus is the reverse contagion. His holiness is stronger than our sickness. He took our filth so we could have His purity.

REFLECT

What is the label you have been wearing lately (e.g., ugly, failure, too much)? What does God call you instead?

....

....

....

Faith vs. Proximity. Are you just bumping into Jesus at church, or are you actually connecting with Him? How do you know?

....

....

....

What is one embarrassing struggle you have been hiding from God? (Hint: He already knows. He's just waiting for you to talk about it).

....

....

....

MICROHABIT

- ❐ Catch yourself every time you mentally label yourself with a negative name ("I'm so awkward," "I'm ugly," "I'm a mess"). Immediately stop the thought. Visualize yourself ripping off that name tag and replacing it with one that says "DAUGHTER." Say out loud: "No, that is not my name. I am a daughter of the King." Retrain your brain to accept your new identity.

MY AFFIRMATION

I am a daughter of the King, and I refuse to be defined by my past or circumstances. I have the spiritual tenacity to press through every obstacle or distraction to receive what God has for me. I am beloved and accepted, and I go in peace knowing my identity is secure! Hallelujah!

Get More

Luke 8:43-48, Mark 5:25-34

CHAPTER 23

Mary Magdalene

JESUS BRINGS TRUE FREEDOM

But you are a chosen generation, a royal priesthood, a holy nation, His own special people, that you may proclaim the praises of Him who called you out of darkness into His marvelous light.

1 Peter 2:9

Magdala was a wealthy fishing town, but for Mary, it had been a living hell.

She remembered the darkness. It wasn't just a bad mood or a depressive episode; it was an occupation. Seven demons. Seven distinct voices of chaos that had hijacked her mind, tormented her body, and isolated her from everyone she loved. She had been the crazy woman of the village. The one people crossed the street to avoid. The one parents used to scare their children. *Stay away from her, or you'll end up like Mary.*

She had been completely lost. A prisoner in her own skin.

And then, Jesus came.

He didn't scream. He didn't use magic potions. He simply spoke, and the darkness fled. He evicted the tenants of hell from her soul and gave her back her mind. For the first time in years, she heard silence. She felt peace.

From that moment on, Mary was all in. She didn't go back to her old life of comfort. She followed Him. She joined the band of disciples. She was wealthy, and she used her resources to fund the ministry. She bought the food, paid for the lodging, and supported the men who would change the world. This was financial stewardship in action.

But her greatest test wasn't her wallet, but her loyalty.

Jerusalem. The Passover. The trial. The Cross.

When the soldiers arrested Jesus, most of the brave men ran for their lives. Only John remained. But Mary stayed, refusing to leave the side of her Deliverer.

She stood at the foot of the cross, watching the Man who saved her die by inches. She heard the hammer blows. She saw the blood. Her heart was breaking, but she refused to leave Him. Loyalty when it's hard means staying when it's dangerous.

Sunday morning. It was dark. The city was asleep. Mary was walking to the tomb, her arms full of spices. She wanted to honor His body one last time.

She found the stone rolled away. Panic set in. After alerting the others, she remained in the garden alone, weeping. Through her tears, she saw a figure. She thought it was the gardener.

"Sir, if You have carried Him away, tell me where You have laid Him."

"Mary."

One word. His voice. The voice that had cast out the demons. The voice that had restored her life.

She spun around. "Rabboni!"

She fell at His feet. He was alive. The nightmare was over. And then, Jesus gave her a commission that would shatter social norms forever. He didn't tell Peter first. He didn't tell John. He told the woman with the dark past.

"Go to My brethren and say to them, 'I am ascending to My Father and your Father.'"

Mary Magdalene ran. Her lungs burned, her hair was a mess, but her spirit was soaring. She burst into the room where the men were hiding.

"I have seen the Lord!"

She was the first evangelist. The first human being in history to preach the Gospel of the Resurrection.

THE DOWNLOAD

There is a nasty rumor that Mary Magdalene was a prostitute. The Bible actually never says that. It says she had seven demons. She had a traumatic, dark, spiritual history.

Her story screams one thing: Your past doesn't disqualify you. Jesus didn't look at her resume and say, "Sorry, too much baggage. You have a history of mental instability. You're a liability." He looked at her and saw a warrior. If you have a dark past, addiction, self-harm, sexual sin, or mental health struggles, Jesus wants to use you. No addiction or darkness is too strong for Jesus. If He could break seven demons off Mary, He can break the chain of anxiety or pornography off you.

I love her loyalty. It's easy to be a Christian at a worship concert when the lights are cool and everyone is singing. It's hard to be a Christian when Jesus gets you mocked at school. Mary stayed at the cross when the boys ran away. Be that girl.

We must also recognize her financial stewardship. Mary was a funder of the Master's ministry. Luke 8:3 tells us she supported Jesus "out of her substance." You are not limited to serving in the background; you can be the financial engine that propels the Gospel forward.

Finally, she was the first evangelist. In that culture, a woman's testimony wasn't even valid in court. Jesus deliberately chose a woman to validate His resurrection. He entrusted the most important message in history to her voice. He values your voice. Do not let anyone silence what God has told you to speak.

MESSIANIC THREAD Mary Magdalene mistook Jesus for the Gardener. It was a beautiful mistake because He is the New Gardener. The first Adam ruined the world in a garden; the Second Adam (Jesus) resurrected in a garden to restore the world.

REFLECT

Do you feel like your past mistakes make you damaged goods? Write down why that is a lie based on Mary's story.

....

....

....

When was the last time you stood up for Jesus when it was awkward or scary?

....

....

....

Mary was the first to tell the Good News. Who is one person you can invite to church or share a verse with this week?

....

....

....

MICROHABIT

- [ ] Start practicing stewardship. If you have an allowance or a job, prayerfully set aside a specific percentage (even if it's $5) to give to your church or a ministry you believe in.

MY AFFIRMATION

I am a carrier of the Good News. I have been delivered from the power of darkness and translated into the Kingdom of Light. I am a faithful steward of the resources God has given me, using my substance to advance His work. I possess the courage to stand with Jesus even when the world mocks Him. I have seen the Lord, and I will not be silent about His power! Hallelujah!

Get More

Luke 8:1-3, John 20:1-18, Mark 16:9

CHAPTER 24

Paul

TRUE PURPOSE IS FOUND ONLY IN CHRIST

> *For I am not ashamed of the gospel of Christ, for it is the power of God to salvation for everyone who believes, for the Jew first and also for the Greek.*
>
> ***Romans 1:16***

The road to Damascus was shimmering in the midday heat, but Saul (later Paul) didn't feel the sun. He felt the cold, hard burn of hatred.

He was a hunter. His prey? Christians.

Saul wasn't a bad guy in the eyes of the world. He was the prom king of Judaism. He was a Pharisee of Pharisees, brilliant, educated, and zealous. He thought he was doing God a favor by rounding up these followers of Jesus and throwing them in prison. He had stood there, arms crossed, approving the murder of Stephen. He had blood on his hands, and he slept like a baby.

He was on his way to arrest more women and children. He was powerful. He was feared. He was unstoppable.

BOOM.

A light brighter than the sun knocked him off his horse. He hit the dirt hard. He was blind. His eyes wide open, seeing nothing but white fire.

"Saul, Saul, why are you persecuting Me?"

The voice shook the earth.

"Who are You, Lord?" Saul gasped.

"I am Jesus, whom you are persecuting."

In that split second, Saul's universe imploded. He wasn't the hero; he was the villain. The Man he thought was a dead heretic was the living God.

This was a radical transformation. God took the person who hated Him the most and turned him into the person who loved Him the most. He stepped out of his identity as Saul the Pharisee and fully embraced his mission as Paul the Apostle, becoming all things to all men that he might save some.

Fast forward thirty years.

The man who used to travel with an entourage and arrest warrants was now sitting in a cold, damp Roman dungeon. Chains chafed his wrists. He was scarred from beatings, shipwrecks, and stonings. He had gone from a VIP to a prisoner.

But look at his face. He isn't bitter. He isn't panicking. He is scribbling a letter to his young mentee, Timothy.

"I have learned in whatever state I am, to be content," he writes. "I know how to be abased, and I know how to abound."

This is contentment that comes from a reborn spirit. Paul wasn't born chill. He had found out that Jesus was enough. He didn't need the status, the comfort, or the freedom to be okay.

He looked at the Roman soldiers chained to him. Paul didn't cower. He preached to them. He wasn't ashamed of the Gospel, because he knew it was the power of God.

He dipped his quill again. He poured his heart out to Timothy. "Let no one despise your youth," he encouraged. Paul understood mentorship. He knew he wouldn't live forever, so he poured everything he knew into the next generation.

As the executioner's date drew near, Paul didn't regret the switch. He didn't wish he was back in his old life of power and comfort. He wrote his final status update:

"I have fought the good fight, I have finished the race, I have kept the faith."

THE DOWNLOAD

Paul is the proof that no one is too far gone. Maybe you know someone, or are someone, who hates God, mocks Christians, or is deep in sin. Paul was a murderer. And God saved him. Radical transformation is God's specialty.

But Paul's story isn't just about conversion; it's about how to live after. The biggest lesson for us in our day is contentment. Paul said he learned it. That means it doesn't come naturally. We have to learn how to be happy without the new iPhone, without the boyfriend, without the latest fashion trend. Contentment is realizing that Christ is sufficient.

Paul models unapologetic boldness. He stood before kings, governors, and angry mobs without flinching. He refused to be ashamed of the Gospel because he understood its value as the power of God unto salvation. We must shed the fear of man. If Paul could preach in chains, we can certainly speak the truth in our daily lives.

Finally, Paul teaches us about perseverance. The Christian life is a marathon, not a sprint. Paul's final words were not about how successful he was, but about how he finished. "I have fought the good fight, I have finished the race." There will be seasons where you want to quit, but the prize is not for the swift; it is for the faithful.

MESSIANIC THREAD Paul calls himself the chief of sinners, yet God made him the primary author of the New Testament. It mirrors the Cross: The worst thing that ever happened (the murder of Jesus) became the best thing that ever happened (the salvation of the world). God takes our worst and redeems it for His best.

REFLECT

Is there anyone you think is too bad for God to save? Pray for them by name today, remembering Paul.

I have learned to be content. On a scale of 1-10, how content are you right now? What is stealing your peace?

....

....

....

Who is a Timothy in your life? Who is a younger girl or new believer you can encourage?

....

....

....

MICROHABIT

- ❒ The next time you catch yourself complaining (about your clothes, your food, your parents), stop mid-sentence. Force yourself to say, "But I have Jesus, and that is enough." Re-train your mind to see what you have, not what you lack.

MY PRAYER

I am unashamed of the Gospel of Jesus Christ, for it is the power of God working in me. I possess the mind of Christ and the endurance of a finisher. I have learned the secret of contentment; my peace is not tied to my circumstances, my status, or my bank account. I run my race with purpose, looking away from distractions and fixing my eyes on the Prize. I am a vessel of mercy, transformed by grace to impact my generation. Hallelujah!

Get More

Acts 9:1-19, Philippians 4:11-13, 2 Timothy 4:7

CHAPTER 25

Jesus

THE VOICE THAT HEALS

> *Let no corrupt word proceed out of your mouth, but what is good for necessary edification, that it may impart grace to the hearers.*
>
> **Ephesians 4:29**

The air in the upper room was suffocating, but not because of the heat. It was the tension. The disciples were at it again: bickering, posturing, throwing sharp words like daggers across the low table.

"I have been with Him the longest!"

"But I sit at His right hand!"

"You don't understand the Kingdom like I do."

Their words were designed to cut. They were designed to elevate themselves by pushing someone else down. It was the exact opposite of everything He had taught them for three years.

Jesus sat in the center of the storm. He knew what was coming. In less than twenty-four hours, His body would be broken, His blood poured out. The weight of the world's sin was pressing on His chest like a physical stone. If anyone had a right to demand silence, comfort, or a little bit of pampering, it was Him. If anyone had a right to snap, "Shut up, all of you!" it was the Son of God.

But He didn't.

He looked at them. He saw their insecurity masked as arrogance. He saw their fear disguised as pride.

He knew that His hour had come. Motivated by a love that persisted despite their pride, Jesus stood up. The room went quiet, the argument dying in their throats. They watched, confused, as He removed His outer garment. This was the Rabbi. The King. The Messiah. And He was stripping down to the dress of a slave.

He poured water into a basin. The sound of the splashing water was the only noise in the room. He knelt.

He took the dirty, calloused, road-weary foot of a disciple into His hands. He didn't recoil at the grime. He washed it.

This was servant leadership in its purest, most shocking form. True greatness was seen as he knelt on the floor, touching the parts of people that everyone else avoided.

When He got to Peter, the big fisherman pulled back. "Lord, You shall never wash my feet!"

Jesus looked up. His eyes were pools of absolute truth, yet there was no condemnation in them. Love in communication was His native tongue. He spoke truth, "If I do not wash you, you have no part with Me," but the intent was to save, not to destroy. He wasn't debating Peter to win an argument; He was speaking to heal Peter's pride.

He moved down the line. He washed John's feet. He washed Thomas's feet. He even washed Judas's feet, the feet that would walk out into the night to betray Him. He treated the traitor with the same dignity as the beloved.

As He worked, the atmosphere in the room shifted. The arrogance evaporated. The disciples weren't left feeling worthless or scolded; they were left feeling challenged and deeply, painfully loved. People shouldn't leave you deflated; after an encounter with Jesus, you left changed.

He finished. He put His robe back on and sat down.

"Do you know what I have done to you?" He asked softly. "If I then, your Lord and Teacher, have washed your feet, you also ought to wash one another's feet."

It wasn't just about feet. It was about how they treated people. Throughout His ministry, He had shattered every social norm. He had engaged women in deep theological debates when other rabbis wouldn't even look at them. He had respected the intellect of the Samaritan woman and the devotion of Mary. He practiced boundaries with compassion, knowing when to withdraw to the mountains to pray so He could return to the crowds with full strength.

He looked around the circle. He had modeled the perfect way to be human. He didn't use His voice to dominate, and He didn't use His power to control. He used His power to serve, and His voice to wash them clean.

THE DOWNLOAD

We have reached the end of the book, and there is no one else to end with but Jesus.

Now, here is a disclaimer: There are infinite aspects of Jesus. He is the Lion, the Lamb, the Healer, the Judge, the King, the Savior. He is so complete that all the books in the world couldn't contain Him. But as we close this book, there is one specific aspect we need to focus on, because it affects every single day of your life: the importance of good communication.

Communication is how we connect, and Jesus was the Master Communicator.

Think about how you talk to your friends, your parents, or even people you think you don't like. Do you use truth as a weapon? Love in communication means asking, "Am I saying this to help them, or to hurt them?" Jesus always spoke to heal. Even when He was correcting the Pharisees, He was trying to wake them up.

Here is a check for you: People shouldn't leave you deflated. Have you ever hung out with someone and left feeling ugly, stupid, or exhausted? Don't be that girl. When people walked away from Jesus, whether it was a rich man or a poor widow, they left feeling seen. They might have been convicted, but they were never worthless.

And girls, notice how He treated us. In a time when women were property, Jesus taught them, defended them, and revealed His resurrection to them first. He gave women equal intellectual and spiritual respect. You don't have to dumb yourself down for anyone. Jesus isn't expecting you to.

Jesus models boundaries. He frequently withdrew to "desolate places" to pray. He understood that you cannot pour from an empty vessel. If the Son of God needed to disconnect from the demands of the crowd to connect with the Father, how much more do we?

Jesus pioneers what servant leadership looks like. The world equates power with being served. The Kingdom equates power with serving. Kingdom greatness is not found on a stage or in a title; it is found in the willingness to do the unseen work. It is treating the unseen person with the same honor as the celebrated one.

MESSIANIC THREAD Every story in this book, from Eve to Paul, points here. The Scarlet Cord of Rahab, the Lamb of Abraham, it is all Him. He is the hero of every story. And He wants to be the hero of yours.

REFLECT

People shouldn't leave you deflated. Be honest: How do people usually feel after a 30-minute conversation with you? Encouraged or drained?

....

....

....

Jesus had boundaries. What is one boundary you need to set (with your phone, a friend, or your schedule) to protect your time with God?

....

....

....

In what ways do you feel Jesus "washing your feet" (serving/loving you) right now in your life?

....

....

....

MICROHABIT

- ❒ Before you send a text, post a comment, or say something about someone this week, run it through three gates: 1. Is it True? 2. Is it Kind? 3. Is it Necessary? If it doesn't pass all three, delete it. Use your voice only to heal, not to harm.

MY PRAYER

Lord Jesus, I acknowledge You as the Author and Finisher of my faith. Thank You for modeling what true love looks like. I thank you for the grace to emulate You. Guard my tongue so that I speak only what is good for edification. Soften my heart to serve those around me without seeking recognition. I surrender my life to Your lordship, asking that You would be the Hero of my story today and forever. Amen.

Get More

John 13:1-17

Why This Book?

The purpose of this book was never just to tell you stories about people who lived thousands of years ago. The purpose was to introduce you to the person who holds all of history together: Jesus. We have traced His Messianic Thread through the lives of broken heroes, unexpected queens, and weary travelers, but truly, this does not even scratch the surface of His glory. Scripture declares in the book of John that Jesus is the Word. He is the logic, the reason, and the power behind everything that exists.

As you read this book you discovered the reality of God and His immense love and care of you.

But this reality goes beyond the pages of a book. Apart from seeing Jesus in the written Word, you must understand that all of creation was created by Jesus. He is the Architect of the universe. This means that everything in the world responds to His voice and finds its true purpose only in Him. A creation cannot function properly until it is connected to its Creator.

That includes you.

You were not an accident; you were designed by the Word, Jesus Christ. The day you discover the bliss that is Jesus is the day you stop merely existing and start truly living. Throughout these chapters, we have watched Jesus give people their lives back, turning shame into glory and emptiness into overflow. Today, that same offer is on the table for you. You can receive the abundant and eternal right now by believing in Jesus and confessing that He is Lord, just as God promised in Romans 10:10.

If you are ready to step into your purpose, pray this prayer to God right now:

Lord God, I believe with all my heart in Jesus Christ, Son of the living God. I believe He died for me and God raised Him from the dead. I believe He's alive today. I confess with my mouth that Jesus Christ is the Lord of my life from this day. Through Him and in His Name, I have eternal life; I'm born again. Thank you, Lord, for saving my soul! I'm now a child of God. Hallelujah!

Congratulations! Welcome to a life of bliss. Welcome to the family of God. The old you is gone; the new you has arrived.

Now, you have access to the same power and identity as the women and men you just read about.

- You can stand with boldness like Esther, knowing you were created for such a time as this.
- You can walk in excellence like Daniel, refusing to compromise with the culture around you.
- You can claim your identity like The Woman with the Issue of Blood, no longer defined by your struggle, but defined by your status as a Daughter.

Your story has just begun.

God bless you!

Made in United States
Cleveland, OH
20 January 2026